The Children's Bible

ILLUSTRATED EDITION

Sally Ann Wright

How to use this book

Here are 365 stories or passages, each accompanied by a thought or question to help both children and adults engage with the message of the Bible and how it might encourage us in our day-to-day lives.

The book can be used as a daily devotional, each meditation being completed with a short prayer which can be used as it is or to build on as families pray together; or it can be read alone as a way of starting or ending the day with God. You could read from the beginning at number 1 and end with 365 or read whole stories or themes together using the index at the back.

Reading the Bible individually or together, whether we are younger or older, larger or smaller families, helps us to know God better and understand what he wants for our lives.

This illustrated book makes reading the Bible easier and more accessible, bringing together sometimes many chapters of a Bible book to help our understanding.

Although both stories and Bible passages are rewritten for a younger readership, they are based on real translations and always referenced to the passages where the original story can be found. Some passages come from the experience of believers like Job or the Psalmists who cried out to God, or who wrote of their experiences of living out the Christian faith in the epistles.

By talking together about our fears, worries or doubts or the happy events that make up our lives, we can share our knowledge and experiences of God together.

Milestones

Name ....

Event & date ....

Name ....

Event & date ....

Name ....

Event & date ....

Name ....

Event & date ....

Name ....

Event & date ....

Name ....

Event & date ....

Children are a gift from the Lord. They are a real blessing.

Psalm 127:3

Milestones

Name ....

Event & date ....

Name ....

Event & date ....

Name ....

Event & date ....

Name ....

Event & date ....

Name ....

Event & date ....

Name ....

Event & date ....

Don't let the excitement of youth cause you to forget your Creator... Love God and do what he tells you to do.

Ecclesiastes 12:1, 13

Special events

For everything there is a season, a time for every activity under heaven.

Ecclesiastes 3:1

Event & date ....

Event & date ....

Event & date ....

Event & date ....

Event & date ....

Event & date ....

Event & date ....

Event & date ....

Event & date ....

Event & date ....

Event & date ....

Event & date ....

Event & date ....

Event & date ....

Event & date ....

Event & date ....

Event & date ....

Event & date ....

Event & date ....

Event & date ....

Event & date ....

Event & date ....

Event & date ....

Event & date ....

Special events

A time to cry and a time to laugh. A time to grieve and a time to dance.

Ecclesiastes 3:4

CONTENTS

1 .... What is life?
2 .... Knowing God
3 .... What is the purpose of life?
4 .... Happy families
5 .... Friendship
6 .... Kindness to the poor is an act of worship
7 .... How much do we want to know God?
8 .... Our great creator God
9 .... Are we taking good care of Gods' world?
10 ...... Isn't it amazing that God cares about you and me?
11 ...... Made to be God's friends
12 ...... Are you easily tempted to do wrong things?
13 ...... What do you do when you feel guilty?
14 ...... Taking responsibility for the choices we make
15 ...... Is it always easy to do the right thing?
16 ...... Are you a rule keeper or a rule breaker?
17 ...... God is our hiding place
18 ...... Who is Jesus?
19 ...... Will God be kind to me?
20 ...... Who is the Holy Spirit?
21 ...... What does the Holy Spirit do?
22 ...... Is the Bible important?
23 ...... How does God speak to us?
24 ...... Should God's timing be the same as ours?
25 ...... Believing the unbelievable
26 ...... Are we ready to accept God's will for us?
27 ...... Are we keen to share with others what God has done for us?
28 ...... Where do we fit in God's plan?
29 ...... Do we sometimes have doubts?
30 ...... Can Jesus understand our fears and weaknesses?
31 ...... God gave the news of Jesus' birth first to ordinary working people.
32 ...... How did you feel when you first met Jesus?
33 ...... Does knowing Jesus bring us joy?
34 ...... Following the truth
35 ...... Do we try to make ourselves seem kinder than we really are?
36 ...... What gifts can we offer to Jesus?
37 ...... Can you imagine what it's like to be a refugee?
38 ...... Why do parents worry?
39 ...... Do we enjoy spending time with God?
40 ...... Does God have a plan for us?
41 ...... Being God's friends
42 ...... Is there someone you really don't like?
43 ...... Doing what God wants
44 ...... Does God's love shine out in our lives?
45 ...... Do you look forward to meeting Jesus?
46 ...... God sees our heart
47 ...... Do you love to give?
48 ...... Being different
49 ...... Trusting God
50 ...... When disaster strikes
51 ...... Are you surprised when God keeps his promises?
52 ...... When God wants you to act…
53 ...... God's plan for Abraham
54 ...... Do you find it hard to wait?
55 ...... God gives strength when we feel weak
56 ...... God keeps his promises
57 ...... Be welcoming to strangers
58 ...... How much do we care about justice?
59 ...... How far would you go to protect someone in need?
60 ...... Mixing with the wrong crowd
61 ...... Abraham's trust in God
62 ...... What would you give up for God?
63 ...... Abraham's faith
64 ...... When you need guidance
65 ...... Do we thank God for answered prayers?
66 ...... Parents aren't perfect…
67 ...... How to be a happy family
68 ...... God's family
69 The importance of love
70 ...... Is your family perfect?
71 ...... Parents and children
72 ...... Have you ever told a lie?
73 ...... Have you ever stolen anything?
74 ...... What should we do when our relationships are spoiled?
75 ...... God's incredible love

76......Can we say that the living God is also our God?
77......God is good
78......The strength of love
79......How do you deal with big disappointments?
80......The ups and downs of life
81......Could people describe us as selfish?
82......Are there broken relationships in your life you have never fixed?
83......Do you get angry easily?
84......We gain nothing by worrying…
85......The blessings and the bad stuff
86......The blessings of God
87......God is beyond understanding
88......Have you ever wanted to run away from God?
89......Prophets aren't perfect
90......Putting others first
91......In God's safe hands
92......Do we pray only when things go wrong?
93......What makes us afraid to tell people about God?
94......What being sorry means
95......Have you ever wanted to get someone into trouble?
96......Do you ever wish that you were someone else?
97......Could you hate someone enough to wish them harm?
98......How well do you know yourself?
99......Do you fall apart when things go wrong or try to make the best of it?
100....The right place and the right time
101....Watching and waiting
102....Our place in the puzzle
103....Are we changed for the better by difficult situations?
104....Do you believe God has plans for your life?
105....Are you ever tempted to take revenge on those who hurt you?
106....Do you know what it is like to feel guilty?
107....Do we doubt that God is taking care of us?
108....How far would you go to protect someone you love?
109....Do you remember still someone who has hurt you in some way?
110....God knows our weaknesses
111....Families matter
112....The God who loves to give
113....When love goes cold
114....Come to God!
115....The God of all the earth
116....Belonging to God
117....Taste and see that God is good
118....Be honest in all you do…
119....Do we trust God for the future?
120....When bad things happen…
121....How does God guide us?
122....Everyone is different
123....Do two wrongs make a right?
124....When there's a turn in the road
125....When God speaks…
126....God needs us!
127....When obedience causes pain
128....God is patient
129....How well do we know God?
130....Do we love God because he is good or because we are afraid?
131....How many chances do we need to trust God?
132....How do we feel when things around us change?
133....When we are afraid…
134....Are we people who grumble?
135....Do we trust God to provide for us daily?
136....How can we live the way God wants us to?
137....How can we show God how much we love him?
138....God knows what we are like

139....How quickly do we forget our good intentions?
140....Are you on God's side?
141....God offers us choices
142....Keeping our side of the agreement
143....The leap of faith
144....Do we want to fit in with the crowd?
145....Is it enough to say sorry?
146....Jesus was no ordinary man
147....Do we give in too easily?
148....Is Jesus interested in all the events in our lives?
149....Life in all its fullness
150....Do we listen to God even when we don't like what he is saying?
151....Will you come and follow me?
152....How can we help people to meet Jesus?
153....Why did Jesus heal people?
154....If Jesus were coming to your street today – would you want to be there?
155....Thoughts and actions
156....Treating people kindly
157....Being good in secret…
158....How should I pray?
159....Should I keep praying for the same thing?
160....Do you ever worry?
161....Do you believe God cares for you?
162....God's way or the world's way?
163....Listen to God
164....God gives us strength and encouragement
165....Do you judge people by where they come from?
166....The power of God
167....Using our common sense
168....Counting our blessings
169....Do you ever feel that what you need to do is too hard?
170....Are you good at keeping promises?
171....Sharing your faith?
172....Do you find it easy to listen to God?
173....How willing are we to do what God asks?
174....Does God have a job for you?
175....How strong is your faith?
176....The right people for the right job
177....Is everything we do done to please God?
178....Do we forget the good things God has done for us?
179....What are your weaknesses?
180....Do you find it hard to be unselfish?
181....Do what is right
182....What would Jesus do?
183....Does God care more about what we believe or what we do?
184....None of us knows what the future holds
185....How loyal are we to those we love?
186....Is God guiding our steps today?
187....God's care and protection
188....Does God have plans for good?
189....God's everlasting love
190....Are we always willing to help others?
191....Amazing faith

192....Do we care about people the way that God does?
193....The gift of God's forgiveness
194....Putting God first
195....Trusting God
196....Do we ask God to help others?
197....The difference that Jesus makes
198....What is God's love like?
199....Is knowing Jesus worth telling others about?
200....Have you ever done something wrong?
201....The importance of hope
202....Do we sometimes make bargains with God?
203....When prayers are answered…
204....Do we expect God to speak to us?
205....Do we believe God wants what is best for us?
206....Do we want to be like everyone else?
207....Asking for guidance
208....How would you respond if God called you to a huge task?
209....The power to change
210....God does not give up on us
211....Do you always want things your own way?
212....Do we judge people by how they look?
213....The God of surprises
214....God's goodness
215....What will heaven be like?
216....The difference that faith makes
217....Is our faith more than just words?
218....Do we trust God to help us?
219....Does knowing God bring us joy?
220....Have you ever wanted something that belongs to someone else?
221....Do you find it easy to admit to mistakes you have made?
222....Can you be honest when you talk to God?
223....Are you ever afraid God will turn his back on you?
224....Learning to forgive yourself.
225....What is God like?
226....What does God need to forgive in your life?
227....How does God bless people who put him first?
228....Do we use the gifts God gives us?
229....Where does God live?
230....Putting others first
231....Do you find it hard to trust Jesus?
232....How do I show that I love God?
233....Should I help anyone who needs me?
234....I am better than you!
235....Learning to forgive
236....How is Jesus like a good Shepherd?
237....Have you ever felt so lost that you don't think even God cares about you?
238....The huge kindness of God
239....Do you mean what you say?
240....Treasure in heaven
241....What does God want from us?
242....What matters most in life?
243....What happens when we do something we're ashamed of?
244....Spending time with God
245....Who does God welcome into his kingdom?
246....How often do we thank God?
247....What kind of person are you?
248....Can we live for ever?
249....Does Jesus care when we suffer?
250....Do we make time for people?
251....Is there something coming between us and God?
252....What stops us asking God for help?
253....When Zacchaeus met Jesus, his whole life changed.
254....God always gives us another chance
255....God takes cares of his children
256....Taking God at his word
257....It's your fault!
258....Choose whom you will worship!
259....God is great!

260....Have you ever felt no one understands you?
261....Do you respect those older than you?
262....Are there limits to our kindness to others?
263....Do we try to earn God's mercy?
264....Who does God choose to serve him?
265....God knows us
266....Something beautiful for God
267....How do we react when we hear God's words?
268....Dark days, dark nights
269....Do we have a sense of purpose?
270....Do we stand up for those with no voice?
271....No limits
272....Are we good at making the best of a bad situation?
273....Does accepting God's blessings mean we don't have to try?
274....Dreams and visions
275....Why does God give us gifts?
276....How do we feel when God answers our prayers?
277....Do we take seriously what God tells us?
278....Do we believe God can work miracles?
279....How much do we value sacred things?
280....If God tested us, what would he find?
281....Have you ever been jealous of what someone else has?
282....Could you be flattered into making a bad choice?
283....Do you think God can be trusted?
284....Can God work through people who don't share our faith?
285....Learning to wait…
286....Do you pray for your leaders?
287....What is worship?
288....What will happen at the end of time?
289....What will make God disappointed with us?
290....How do the things we say and do show what we are really like?
291....Are we more likely to follow a great hero or someone who is good and kind?
292....Real religion – or just for show?
293....How much are we prepared to give back to God?
294....When friends let you down…
295....The servant king
296....Could I be the one who betrays Jesus?
297....Is there room for everyone in heaven?
298....How can we do things that really matter?
299....What difference does the Holy Spirit make?
300....Remember me
301....Don't think of yourselves!
302....Jesus' struggle

303....The kiss of betrayal
304....True friends?
305....Have you ever let someone down badly?
306....When good men do nothing…
307....Jesus' suffering
308....Can anyone be forgiven?
309....Thinking of others
310....The humility of Jesus
311....Are we only Christians on Sundays?
312....Knowing Jesus
313....Who do we want to be?
314....Why did Jesus die?
315....Taking risks for Jesus
316....Do you share what you learn with others?
317....Seeing is believing…
318....Jesus changes everything
319....Meeting Jesus…
320....Do you enjoy being with other believers?
321....Does Jesus make a difference in your life?
322....Jesus understands us
323....Do you like to wait?
324....Am I good enough to go to heaven?
325....What it means to be a Christian
326....One big family
327....Have you ever said something you shouldn't have?
328....The power to do good
329....Peter, a changed person
330....More than we ask for…
331....Unexpected results
332....Is good news not worth sharing?
333....Living the way Jesus taught
334....The truth hurts
335....When people are sure they are right…
336....Do we use every opportunity God gives us?
337....God needs us!
338....What things do we do that hurt Jesus?
339....The way prayer works
340....When trusting God is hard…
341....What happens when we meet Jesus?
342....Taking things to God in prayer
343....Faith leads to kind actions
344....The power of praying people
345....Does God have favourites?
346....Do you value your freedom to worship God?
347 Are we ready for the answers God gives us?
348....Can you praise God even when things go badly?
349....Have you ever told a stranger about your faith?
350....Would you give up if people laughed at you for your faith?
351....How easy is it for you to trust God?
352....Are you ready to share God's love with people you meet today?
353....What matters more to you than anything else?
354....How can we show God we love him?
355....All working together
356....We need each other
357....What is the most important gift?
358....What does real love look like?
359....Can people see Jesus in us?
360....What does God want?
361....How can we show that God is in our lives?
362....How does God treat us like his children?
363....Have you ever wanted to give up?
364....How much do we love God?
365....Keep on keeping on…

What is life?

Solomon searched for its meaning and learned to trust God.

📖 Ecclesiastes 3:1-13

There is a right time for everything: a time to be born; a time to die; a time to plant; a time to harvest; a time to kill; a time to heal; a time to destroy; a time to rebuild; a time to cry; a time to laugh; a time to grieve; a time to dance; a time to hug; a time not to hug; a time to find; a time to lose; a time for keeping; a time for throwing away; a time to tear; a time to repair; a time to be quiet; a time to speak up; a time for loving; a time for hating; a time for war; a time for peace.

What do we gain from all that we do on earth? God has planted eternity in our hearts — we know that this life is not all there is — and yet we cannot see what God sees, the beginning and the end.

We should learn to be happy with what we have and enjoy all the gifts that God gives us.

Help us to be happy with the life we have, and trust you for the future which we cannot see.

2

Lord, we want you to be our friend now. We want you to be our friend every day.

Knowing God

King Solomon encouraged people to give their lives to God while they were still young.

📖 *Ecclesiastes 12:1-8*

Get to know God while you are still young. Let God be your friend throughout your whole life.

Don't wait till you are old and tired and need help to do things. Don't wait till you are too weak to enjoy life any more. Don't wait till you are on your death bed…

Instead enjoy a relationship with your Creator while you are still active and enthusiastic and can spend your life doing the good things God wants you to do. Then you will be able to look back and know that your life has been worthwhile.

What is the purpose of life?

King Solomon believed it was to love God and keep his commandments.

 Ecclesiastes 12:13-14

When Solomon was an old man, he looked back over his life. He had been a wise man. God had given him money and property, power and long life. He had learned a lot over his many years on earth.

The advice he gave to others was simple.

'Love and respect God and obey his commandments. Nothing else matters. Everything else seems pointless; it has no lasting value.

'For God sees everything we do, including the things we do in secret. He weighs up the good things and the bad things. Don't let him down.

'Love God, for this is the best way to live; it is why we are here.'

We want to have purpose in our lives, Lord. Let us each love you with all of our hearts.

4 Happy families

What was Solomon's secret for a happy family?

📖 Proverbs

Teach us to be good parents who care for our children; teach us to be good children who respect our parents.

'Listen to what your parents tell you,' Solomon advised. 'Their teaching will build good character in the same way as good clothes make you look smart.

'A wise child pays attention when parents correct him, but a foolish one never admits that he is wrong.

'If you love your children, you will correct them when they are naughty.

'The start of an argument is like a hole in a dam. Stop it quickly before it gets out of control.

'There is nothing sadder than a parent whose child does foolish things.

'Discipline your children while they are young enough to learn or they will destroy themselves.

'Children are lucky if they have a father who is honest and does what is right.

'Stealing from your parents is never right.'

Friendship

Solomon was a great believer in kindness and forgiveness.

 *Proverbs*

'A gentle answer can turn anger away, but a cross reply can make things worse.

'It is never good to gossip; it stirs up trouble and breaks up friendships.

'It is better to eat bread and water with your friends than to eat a feast with your enemies.

'If you want people to like you, forgive them when they do something wrong. Remembering wrongs can ruin friendships.

'If you want to stay out of trouble, be careful about what you say.

'Don't make friends with people who have hot tempers. You might learn their habits and find it hard to change.

'A friend means well, even if he hurts you. But if an enemy starts pretending to be your friend, trouble is bound to follow.'

Help us to be good friends to others, Lord, to speak gently, never gossip and to forgive people who hurt us.

Kindness to the poor is an act of worship

Solomon believed in generosity – and in trusting God.

 Proverbs

'Do good to those who are in need whenever you can. Don't tell someone you will help them tomorrow if you can help them today.

'Be generous, and you will do well. Help others and you will be helped.

'If you want to be happy, be kind to the poor. Never belittle other people.

'If you oppress poor people, you insult God who made them; but if you are kind to the poor it's as good as worshipping God in Church.

'Do what is right and fair; that pleases God more than any gift you can offer him.

'Don't wear yourself out trying to get rich. Your money can disappear in a moment as if it had grown wings and flown away.

'It is better to have no money and be honest than to be rich and dishonest.'

Give us a generous spirit, Lord, to share all the good things you have given to us.

How much do we want to know God?

The Psalmist wants to know him more than anything else.

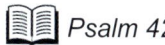 Psalm 42

Just as the deer longs to drink in cool refreshing streams of water, so I long to know you, Lord.

My whole being cries out to you, the living God. When things are difficult for me and people ask me, 'Where is your God now?' I long to worship you, to be where you are, to be in your presence where there is joy and thanksgiving and the company of other believers.

Why am I so sad? What is this struggle within me? I will trust God, my rock. I will tell him I love him. From the deep places inside me, I will reach out for him and know he will help me whatever happens, because he is my God.

When we are struggling, may we long to know you better and trust in your strength to save us.

Our great creator God

Generations of people have been amazed by the natural world. They have seen God's handiwork and praised him for it.

Creator God, you are great and mighty! I love to look at the stars and think about how you made them to sparkle in the night sky. Thank you for the world you have given us.

 *Psalm 19:1-6*

The heavens above us show your glory, Lord. The patterns of the stars, the shape of the moon in the night sky shine out, amazing us with their beauty and demonstrating that a great creator God has made them.

We see the bright sun move across the skies and marvel at it. We love its warmth and see how it gives life to the earth. It makes us happy!

Are we taking good care of God's world?

God made the world with all the good things in it that we need to survive and live well.

📖 *Genesis 1:1-25*

In the very beginning, there was nothing but darkness and chaos.

Then God said, 'Let there be light!'

And there was light – and God saw that it was good.

God went on to make the world we know with rugged mountains and deep valleys, cool streams, flowing rivers and salty seas. God filled the world with leafy trees and flowering plants. God made the hot sun to shine by day and scattered stars around the silvery moon that shone at night.

God made every kind of creature that swims and flies and burrows and gallops. . . striped, spotted, plain and patterned; soft and furry, hard and spiky.

God looked at all that he had made and saw that it was good.

Lord, thank you for the beauty of creation and its harvests of good things for us to eat.

Thank you, Lord, that you are a great creator God — yet you still have time for me.

Isn't it amazing that God cares about you and me?

God is great! He made the whole wide world — and he made us.

 Genesis 1:26-31

God's world was full of sound and colour and variety. But God had not finished yet. God wanted to make people who were more like him — able to be creative, to think and feel and love.

God made them male and female, man and woman, to be his friends.

God gave them his world to look after, from the fish and the birds to creatures that lived on the earth, from the creepy crawlies to the great lumbering beasts.

Made to be God's friends

God made us to be in relationship with him, to know us and for us to know him.

📖 *Genesis 2:8-22*

God gave Adam and Eve – the man and the woman he had made – a beautiful place to live in. It was called the garden of Eden. There was a clear stream with cool water to drink, trees full of delicious fruits to eat and everything that they needed.

Adam gave names to all the animals and together Adam and Eve tended the garden.

God told them they could eat from every tree there except the one in the middle of the garden, the tree of the knowledge of good and evil.

So the people lived there happily with God as their friend. Every day they would talk together.

Lord, I want to be your friend and to talk to you every day. I want to know you and be known by you.

I want to learn to be more like you, able to think and feel and love…

12

Help me to listen to your voice, Lord, and trust you to keep me away from things that might make me hurt myself and others too.

Are you easily tempted to do wrong things?

God made rules to help us do what is right and good.

 Genesis 3:1-5

One day, a serpent spoke to Eve in the Garden of Eden.

'Did God tell you not to eat the fruit from the trees in the garden?' he hissed.

'No, God said we can eat from every tree except from the tree in the middle of the garden,' she replied.

'God knows that if you eat from this tree, you will become as clever as he is,' replied the serpent. 'You will know all that God knows. Look how delicious it looks. Taste it and see…'

What do you do when you feel guilty?

We all know how horrible it is to feel ashamed. But we don't need to hide from God.

 Genesis 3:6-8

Eve saw that the fruit looked ripe and juicy. She liked the idea of knowing as much as God did. Then she reached up and picked a piece of the fruit and took a bite. She shared some with Adam.

Suddenly they were both afraid. Up until that moment they had known only happiness, only good things. But now they realized that what they had done was wrong.

When they heard God coming to talk to them in the evening as he always did, Adam and Eve hid from him. They knew they had disobeyed God. They were ashamed, they felt guilty.

I am sorry when I don't listen to you and do things of which I am ashamed. Thank you that I don't need to hide from you because you love me and are always there for me.

14

Taking responsibility for the choices we make

It's always easier to blame other people but God wants us to be honest about the things we do.

📖 *Genesis 3:8-13, 16-23*

Adam and Eve were hiding from God in the beautiful garden God had given them. They felt guilty and ashamed. God had told them not to do just one thing – and they did it anyway.

'It's Eve's fault,' said Adam. 'She gave me the fruit – I only ate it.'

'It's not my fault,' said Eve. 'The serpent tempted me and I picked it!'

'Now you know the difference between what is good and what is bad, what is right and what is wrong,' said God. 'You have not trusted me to take care of you. Now you must live by the choices you have made.'

Help me to admit when I am in the wrong, Lord. Forgive me when I blame other people for the choices I make.

Is it always easy to do the right thing?

The apostle Paul knew what it was like to struggle against temptation, just as we do.

📖 *Romans 7:15-25*

Paul once wrote a letter to the new Christians in Rome.

'I don't understand myself at all,' he said, 'for I really want to do what is right, but I can't. Sometimes I know that what I am doing is wrong, but I can't help myself – the sin inside me seems to be stronger than I am. I don't do the good things I want to do, and the harder I try, I still find myself doing the wrong things.

'I love God with all my heart, but there is a battle going on inside me. I want to be everything God wants me to be but my old self won't let me go.

'Is there no way out? Of course there is! When Jesus died on the cross and rose again – he set me free from my old self. Praise God for what Jesus has done!'

I know I am not perfect, Lord, and I find it hard sometimes to do what is right. But thank you that Jesus died in my place on the cross and that you have forgiven me for all the wrong things I have ever done.

16

May all that I say and all that I think be pleasing to you, Lord, my rock and my redeemer.

Are you a rule keeper or a rule breaker?

Even if we see rules as helpful, we are all guilty of breaking God's laws.

 Psalm 19:7-13

Your laws are perfect, Lord, helping us decide between right and wrong. Your laws are just and more important to us than riches. They are sweeter than honey dripping from a honeycomb, protecting us and warning us about things that may hurt us.

Help me to see the faults hidden inside me, Lord. Keep me from choosing to do bad things which may lead to even more terrible things.

God is our hiding place

How often do we first turn to God when things go wrong?

 *Psalm 46*

God is our refuge and strength, always there to help when we need him.

Whatever happens to us, or the world around us, we don't need to be afraid because God is always there.

Whatever else fails or goes wrong, God is the same. Where God is, there is peace and when we come to him we can be refreshed and revived and given new strength.

Come and see what God has done. Listen to his voice when he says, 'Be still, and know that I am God'.

God is great and he is with us; the God of all who have gone before us and loved him and known him and trusted him, he is our safe tower, our hiding place in times of trouble.

Thank you that you are God. Help us to be still and know your strength and your peace.

Who is Jesus?

Jesus is God's Son and shows us what God is like.

 Hebrews 1:1-14

In the past God spoke to us through his prophets. Now he speaks through Jesus, his Son. Jesus shows us God himself, his nature and his character. We know what God is like when we know Jesus.

Jesus was there with God when the earth was being made. Yet Jesus was later born into a human family; he became just like us so he could die like us – and by dying he set us free from the fear of death itself. After Jesus had died in our place on the cross, God gave him new life so he was alive when he returned to God's side in heaven, where he is even now.

Jesus is much greater than the angels who are God's servants, there to worship Jesus as they worship God himself – and there to care for the people Jesus died for.

Thank you, Lord Jesus, that you show us what God is like.

Will God be kind to me?

God welcomes us all because of what Jesus has done.

📖 *Hebrews 2:14-18; 4:14-16*

Jesus became human like us, so he understands what makes us afraid and how we suffer. He speaks to God on our behalf and helps us when we find things difficult.

We can be sure that God will welcome us when we come to him because Jesus has gone before us like a priest who speaks for his people. Jesus understands our weaknesses: he was tempted just as we are to do the wrong thing but, unlike us, when he was tempted, he always did the right thing.

We can come to God boldly, knowing that he will be kind to us – not because we are always good but because Jesus is – and he will help us when we need it most.

Thank you so much, Lord, for becoming like us so you know just how we feel.

Who is the Holy Spirit?

The Holy Spirit is God, just as Jesus is also God.

 John 16:1-15

On the night before he died, Jesus talked to his friends, the men with whom he had spent so much time for three years.

'I know you are sad because I am going away,' Jesus said to his friends, 'but good things will happen because of it. When I go, the Holy Spirit, the comforter, will come to you.

'The Holy Spirit will help people understand what sin is – and show them how to be sorry for their sin. The Holy Spirit will teach people that God is good and kind and loving and that there is a way to be forgiven for the bad things in their lives.

'When the Holy Spirit comes he will help you to understand everything and lead you into the truth.'

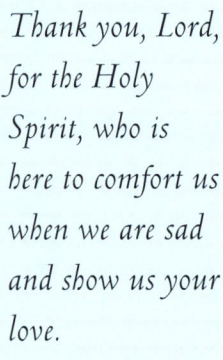

Thank you, Lord, for the Holy Spirit, who is here to comfort us when we are sad and show us your love.

What does the Holy Spirit do?

He speaks for us and helps us in the same way that Jesus did when he lived on earth.

 Romans 8:26-27

When we have faith, the Holy Spirit helps us with the problems we have in our lives, day by day.

    The Holy Spirit also helps us to pray. Sometimes we don't know what we should be praying for, nor the best way to pray – but the Holy Spirit prays with us with such feeling that it goes beyond words. And God the Father, who knows what is inside each of our hearts, knows what the Holy Spirit is saying. In this way the Holy Spirit helps us to work with God to do what is right and good.

Help me now, Lord, as I pray, to tell you all that is in my heart…

Is the Bible important?

The Psalmist believed the Bible was necessary to understand who God is and to guide us how to live.

 Psalm 119:9,15,27,36,103,114

How can a young person do what is right? Surely it is by obeying what we read in the Bible.

Open my eyes, Lord, so that I can see the wonderful truth in your words.

Help me to understand the meaning of all you have taught your children and all the wonderful things you have done.

Help me to be guided by you because I know that will make me happy.

Protect me from things that are worthless so that I may know the meaning of life.

Your words taste sweeter than honey; they are a lamp to guide my feet and a light to show me the way.

Lord, you take care of me and protect me and I find hope in all I read in your word.

Lord, may I learn to love your word and to find in it all I need to follow you with all my heart.

How does God speak to us?

The apostle Paul believed that God spoke through the words of the Bible.

 2 Timothy 3:14-17

Remember all the things I have taught you and act on them. You know that I have suffered for what I believe and you can trust that those things are true.

You were taught to read God's word from childhood and through it you have come to understand that Jesus died for you so that you could live with him in heaven.

All Scripture is inspired by God himself: it is useful to teach us what is true and to help us realize what is wrong in our lives. It corrects us when we are wrong and teaches us to do what is right. God uses it to prepare and train his people to do all the good things needed in his world.

Thank you for the freedom to read your word, Lord, and to hear you speak to us through it.

Should God's timing be the same as ours?

God answered the prayers of Elizabeth and Zechariah when they had decided God's answer must be no.

 Luke 1:5-17

When Herod was king of Judea, God's prophecies about a Saviour for his people began to come true. It started with the priest Zechariah and his wife Elizabeth.

Elizabeth and Zechariah had a great sadness in their life: they had asked God for a child but although they had prayed for many years, they were still without children. Now they were old. Perhaps it was not God's purpose for them to have children?

When it was Zechariah's turn to burn incense in the temple, the angel Gabriel appeared beside the altar.

'Don't be afraid, Zechariah,' said the angel. 'God has heard your prayers. Soon you will be blessed with a baby son. Call him John. God has chosen him to prepare the people for his chosen Saviour, to turn their hard hearts back to faith.'

Give us patience, Lord, to live obediently, trusting that your way is best.

Believing the unbelievable

Would we be more amazed at the presence of the angel or at his message?

25

Teach us, Lord, to see with the eyes of faith and trust you to do great things.

📖 *Luke 1:18-22*

Zechariah was amazed. He could hardly believe the message of the angel.

'Are you sure?' he asked. 'Both my wife and I are old now – probably too old to have children of our own.'

The angel replied, 'I am the angel Gabriel and God has sent me with this message. All this will happen as I have said but as you cannot believe me, until that time you will lose your voice.'

The people outside the temple praying were worried. Zechariah had been inside for a long time. But when he came out, unable to speak, they realized he had seen a vision.

A little while later, Elizabeth told him that she was expecting a baby...

26

Lord, let our love be like Mary's, simple, deep and trusting, knowing that your will is best.

Are we ready to accept God's will for us?

Mary accepted God's plan for her as a gift.

📖 *Luke 1:26-38*

Elizabeth had a young cousin called Mary who was going to marry Joseph, a carpenter. Mary lived in Nazareth in the area around Lake Galilee.

Six months after Gabriel had been to see Zechariah, he went to visit Mary.

'Don't be afraid,' said Gabriel. 'God has chosen to bless you, Mary. You will have a child named Jesus, and he will be called the Son of God himself.'

'But how?' said Mary. 'I don't yet have a husband.'

'Nothing is impossible for God,' said the angel. 'Trust him. Elizabeth is also expecting a baby and everyone said that was impossible too.'

Mary thought for a moment. 'I love God,' she said. 'I am ready to do whatever he wants of me.'

Then the angel Gabriel left Mary.

Are we keen to share with others what God has done for us?

What could we tell someone about God's love today?

 Luke 1:39-45

Mary wanted to tell someone about the angel's message. She thought Elizabeth would understand as she was also going to have a baby. Mary travelled into the hills where Elizabeth lived.

'Hello!' Mary called as she drew near. When Elizabeth heard Mary's voice, the baby inside her kicked with joy!

'I'm so lucky that the mother of the Saviour is here visiting me!' said Elizabeth. 'God has done something very wonderful; and you are amazing, Mary – God has blessed you because he knew you trusted him.'

Mary was so happy that she praised God, telling him how wonderful he was – to choose an ordinary girl to be the mother of his Son.

Thank you, Lord, that we don't have to be the best or the greatest for you to love us or to give us important things to do.

Where do we fit in God's plan?

Each of us has a part to play to make God's will be done.

 Luke 1:57-66

Mary stayed with Elizabeth for three happy months. After she had gone home, Elizabeth gave birth to her own baby son. Just as the angel Gabriel had told them, they named him John.

Zechariah, who had been quiet for so long, then found he could speak once more. Zechariah knew now that his son John was also part of God's plan. John would be the one to tell people that Jesus was coming and prepare them for something amazing to happen.

Help us see what we need to do today to serve you and those around us.

Do we sometimes have doubts?

God will often give us the help and encouragement we need.

 Matthew 1:18-25

Joseph loved Mary. He had planned to marry her; but now she was telling him stories about being visited by an angel. . . and she was pregnant.

Joseph knew it was not his baby but Mary had said she was carrying God's Son. Could her story be true? He was worried people would say unkind things about her.

Then one night Joseph dreamed that an angel spoke to him.

'Don't worry, Joseph. Marry Mary just as you had planned. She needs you to help take care of God's Son.'

When Joseph woke up, he was not so sad any more. God had given him an important job to do.

Lord, increase our faith when we have doubts.

Can Jesus understand our fears and weaknesses?

God's Son came into the world as a helpless baby, born into a poor family in an occupied country.

 *Luke 2:1-7*

Mary and Joseph were not ruled by kings like Saul or David or Solomon – they were now living in a tiny part of the huge Roman empire. Roman soldiers marched about their towns and villages. Their rules were given to them by the Roman Emperor.

Caesar Augustus had issued an order that everyone should return to the place where their families came from to be counted so he could tax them.

So Joseph took Mary with him to Bethlehem, the city where King David had lived long, long ago, because he was a descendant of David.

While they were there, Mary's baby son was born. She wrapped him up warmly and made a bed for him in a manger because there was no room for them to stay in the inn.

Thank you, Lord, that though you are God, you chose to live among us and know how it feels to be human.

God gave the news of Jesus' birth first to ordinary working people.

Does the good news of Jesus make us want to go to worship him?

📖 *Luke 2:8-14*

On that cold, starry night there were shepherds out on the hills, watching over their sheep. Suddenly they were blinded by a bright light in the sky. They shielded their eyes from the strange sight.

'Don't be afraid,' said an angel. 'I am bringing you good news! Jesus, your Saviour, has been born in Bethlehem today. You will find him lying in a manger.'

Then there were hundreds of angels, lighting up the dark night sky. 'Glory to God who lives in heaven and peace to everyone who lives on earth,' they sang.

'We must go and see this wonderful thing that God has told us!' the shepherds said. Then they left their sheep and went to find the baby with the angels' song still echoing in their ears.

Thank you for the good news of Jesus' birth, the gift of a Saviour given for everyone.

How did you feel when you first met Jesus?

Do we want to share the good news with others so they too can know their Saviour?

📖 Luke 2:15-20

Give us joy in our hearts today because we know Jesus, our Saviour and Lord.

The shepherds found the baby in Bethlehem, lying in a manger, just as the angel had promised.

Then they told Mary and Joseph and anyone who would listen about the angels and their message that Jesus, the Saviour, was born! Then they returned to their sheep, praising God.

When they had gone, Mary wondered at all that had happened that night. She had given birth to Jesus, her first baby, a baby promised to her by an angel; a baby who was God's Son, the Saviour of the world. And God had chosen not just to tell her but to share it with others.

Does knowing Jesus bring us joy?

Can people around us see that we know Jesus?

📖 *Luke 2:21-38*

Mary wanted to say thank you to God for the gift of her baby son. She went with Joseph to the temple in Jerusalem, according to the custom, to offer God two pigeons in thanksgiving.

When they arrived an old man named Simeon took the baby in his arms and laughed with joy.

'God told me that I would see the Saviour before I died! And here he is!' he said. 'Now I can die in peace.' But he also warned Mary that there would be some painful times for her in the time to come – not everyone would accept her son.

A prophetess called Anna also saw Mary and Joseph – and she too knew immediately that Jesus had arrived and thanked God, before telling everyone there about him.

Help us to share with everyone we meet today that we know you and love you.

Following the truth

How far would you travel if you believed you would find Jesus there?

📖 Matthew 2:1-2

A new star appeared in the sky when Jesus was born. Far away in eastern lands, wise men, gazing at the stars and studying their positions, believed that it meant that a new king had been born to the Jewish people.

They packed treasure chests and went to worship him, following the star.

When they arrived in Jerusalem, they went to the palace, expecting to find a baby king there. King Herod came to meet them, wondering what their visit could mean.

'Where is the baby born to be king of the Jews?' they asked. 'We have come to worship him.'

Thank you, Lord, that wherever we come from, we can still come to worship you.

Do we try to make ourselves seem kinder than we really are?

Herod said one thing while he was thinking something quite different.

 Matthew 2:3-8

Herod was already king of Judea but he was not a wise or a kind king; he was a cruel and jealous man.

'A baby king?' he thought. 'There is room for only one king here!'

So Herod asked his priests where the prophecies said that a king would be born.

'From Bethlehem,' came the answer.

King Herod listened to the news with growing anger. But he began to form a plan. He returned to greet his visitors, smiling sweetly.

'Go to Bethlehem,' he told them. 'And when you find this special baby, this king of the Jews, please tell me so that I can worship him too. . .'

Let everything I think and say and do be honest and truthful.

What gifts can we offer to Jesus?

What he wants is our love and for us to live thinking first of others.

 Matthew 2:9-12

The wise men made their way to Bethlehem, following the star until it seemed to shine brightly over a little house. They unpacked their gifts and went to the house where they found Jesus with his mother, Mary.

The wise men bowed down low and worshipped Mary's little boy. Then they offered the gifts they had brought from their treasure chests: gold, frankincense and myrrh.

That night, as they slept, God warned them in a dream to return another way. King Herod was already planning how he could harm the little boy they had come to worship.

Lord, we offer our lives to you — please use us to help others.

Can you imagine what it's like to be a refugee?

Jesus understood. Jesus was a child refugee in Egypt, fleeing for his life.

📖 Matthew 2:13-18

An angel appeared to Joseph as he slept and warned him about King Herod's plans.

'Wake up!' he said. 'You must take Jesus and his mother and run away to Egypt. Herod will not rest until he has searched everywhere to find the child. He is already planning how he will have him killed!'

So Joseph woke Mary and told her to prepare for the journey. They did not wait till morning – they made their escape by night, taking Jesus to Egypt and safety.

When Herod realized that the wise men were not coming back, he was so angry that he gave orders for every little boy under two years old to be killed. He wanted to be sure that Jesus could not be king.

There was much weeping and wailing in Bethlehem because of King Herod's wickedness.

Lord, help us to put ourselves in the shoes of others who are not safe in their own homes.

Why do parents worry?

Giving freedom teaches us responsibility but things can, and sometimes do, go wrong.

 Luke 2:41-45

Jesus grew up just as other boys of his age did.

Mary and Joseph taught him how to love God and live by his laws. Most people knew him as Jesus, the carpenter's son.

Every year, Mary and Joseph joined with many other people, travelling from Nazareth to Jerusalem for the Passover festival, a time of singing and praying and parties, celebrating the time when God had led the Israelites out of Egypt.

When Jesus was twelve, Mary and Joseph went to Jerusalem as usual. It was only as they returned with their friends that they realized that neither of them had seen Jesus for a while. They thought he was with the other children but when they found that no one had seen him, they became very anxious. They left the others and hurried back to Jerusalem.

Lord, help us to be good at talking to each other so everyone is kept safe and no one needs to worry.

Do we enjoy spending time with God?

Do we want to get to know God better and to become more like him?

📖 Luke 2:46-52

Mary and Joseph walked the busy streets looking for Jesus. They searched for three days, becoming more anxious with every hour that passed. Where could he be? What could have happened?

Then they went to the temple. There was Jesus, sitting talking with the religious leaders about God.

'Where have you been – we were so worried!' they said.

'I was here all the time, here in my Father's house,' Jesus told them.

Other people may have thought he was the carpenter's son, but Jesus already knew who his Father was.

Thank you that you are our Father too, Lord, that you welcome us into your family. Help us to want to know you better.

40

Does God have a plan for us?

The apostle Paul believed that as members of God's family, we were chosen to do good things.

 Ephesians 2:8-10, 19-22

God's kindness knows no limits. It is because of it that you belong to his family and know that you are saved from your sin. We are not saved from sin as a reward for the good we have done, it is God's gift to us.

God himself made us who we are and gave us new lives; and long ago he planned that we should spend those lives helping others.

You are no longer strangers to God but members of God's own family and you belong in God's home with every other Christian. Together we are joined to Jesus Christ and to each other as day by day our family is growing.

Thank you that we are part of your huge family, Lord. Show us how we can help someone else today.

Being God's friends

We need to be honest with God about who we are.

 1 John 1:5-9

God is light and in him there is no darkness at all. There are no dark corners where bad things can be hidden.

So if we say we are God's friends but then go on living the same old way, doing things that hurt others or only please ourselves, we are lying.

When we live in the light of God's presence as Jesus does, we can know true happiness and know that all our sin has been forgiven and forgotten.

If we say that we are not sinful and have no sin to forgive, we are only fooling ourselves. But if we tell God we are sorry for our sins, he will forgive us – our sin will be washed away. Jesus died on the cross to make this possible.

Lord, there are some dark corners in my life that I need to tell you about…

Is there someone you really don't like?

God calls us to love even the people we find it hard to like.

 1 John 2:3-11

How can we be sure that we belong to Jesus? We need to ask ourselves whether we are really trying to do what God wants us to.

Anyone can say, 'I am a Christian; I am on my way to heaven,' but if we don't do what God wants us to do, how can that be true? We should live as Jesus himself did to show that we belong to him. This is not a new rule but one that Jesus himself taught us: love one another. Then it is as if someone has shone a bright light in our lives. It is good!

If we still hate someone in our hearts or even dislike someone, we are still stumbling around in darkness. Come out into the light! Walk in the light!

Forgive us when we find it hard to like someone. Help us to love others as you love us.

Doing what God wants

How do we show in our lives that God's love is in us?

📖 1 John 3:1-3, 17-18

God loves us so much that he calls us his children – we are really part of his family! And because we are his children we will behave in the way that he does, we will show the same characteristics as our heavenly father.

So if we have enough money to live well and see someone else who is struggling, what should we do? If we do nothing to help, how can God's love be within us?

We must surely stop just saying we love people; we must really love them, and show it by what we do.

Let your love shine out in our lives because we are your children!

Does God's love shine out in our lives?

As we get to know God better, we show the family likeness – we become more like our heavenly father.

📖 1 John 4:7-10

Let us practise loving each other.
    Love comes from God himself and if we are loving and kind, we show in our lives that we are God's children, part of his huge family, and that we are getting to know him better.
    Are you loving and kind? Maybe you need to practise more – and let God's love shine through.
    God showed how much he loved us by sending Jesus, his only son, into the world so that we might live for ever because of his death on the cross. That's real love! It's not our love for God but his love for us – being willing to sacrifice his son for us even before we loved him.

I want to know you better, Lord, so everyone can see I am part of your family.

Do you look forward to meeting Jesus?

When we know we love him and he loves us, we have nothing to be afraid of.

📖 1 John 4:11-17

Since God has loved us so much he let his son die for us, surely we ought to love each other too?

We have not seen God yet but when we love each other, God lives in us, and we become more loving people as his love grows stronger in us.

The Holy Spirit in our hearts is proof that God has made his home in us. It is because of this that we love to tell other people about God's love for us; we love to tell them about Jesus and what he has done for us. And we long for the day when we can meet him face to face.

Thank you, Lord God, for making your home in me.

46

Keep me from being jealous, Lord, so that my jealousy does not lead to something much worse.

God sees our hearts

Cain's jealousy of Abel became an anger so great that he killed his brother…

📖 *Genesis 4:1-12, Hebrews 11:4*

Adam and Eve had two sons, Cain and Abel. Cain and Abel wanted to thank God for taking care of them, giving them good harvests and new-born lambs and kids. Abel chose his best lamb to give to God while Cain gave some of his grain.

God was pleased with Abel's gift because he knew that Abel had come with faith and thanksgiving in his heart. But God knew that Cain had given his gift because he thought he had to. God saw inside his heart.

Cain was so angry with his brother that he attacked him and left him to die. But he couldn't hide what he had done from God.

Do you love to give?

The first Christians used to share all they had to help those who were in most need.

📖 *2 Corinthians 9:6-14*

The apostle Paul wrote to the Christians who lived in Corinth, encouraging them to be generous.

'Give generously, not just because I am asking you to but because you know it's what God wants you to do. Make up your own minds about how much you should give. God loves those who give cheerfully.

'Remember that God gives you everything you need and much more besides – there will always be enough to share with others. Then those you help will know how much God has blessed you and they will praise God – and they will know that your faith is real, not just empty words.'

Help me to be generous, Lord, and to be happy to share what I have with others.

Being different

One of the hardest things we ever have to do is to be willing to be different when others don't seem to care about God.

Genesis 6:5-21

God looked with great sadness at the way the people he had made told lies and cheated and stole from each other. They fought and killed each other. God had made people to be his friends but no one remembered who he was; no one, that is, except Noah.

When God spoke to Noah, Noah listened. God told Noah that soon there would be a great flood that would cover the land. Everything would be destroyed.

'You must build an ark,' God told Noah. 'I will give you instructions for exactly how big it must be and how it should be built. You must collect two each of every animal that I have made so they will be kept safe until after the flood.'

Help me to remember you today, Lord, when others seem to forget. Help me to stand apart if others are being unkind. Help me to listen when you speak to me and to be ready to act.

Trusting God

Has God ever asked you to do something that seems to make no sense?

📖 *Genesis 6:22 – 7:6-10*

Noah's neighbours laughed when they saw him felling cypress trees and cutting them into logs. They made fun of him when they saw the shape of a boat being formed. Surely Noah was a crazy old man! But Noah and his family sawed and hammered, just as God had told them to, until one day, the ark was ready.

It was huge – longer than a football field and higher than a three-storey building. Noah and his family watched as, two by two, animals of every kind came into the ark: lions, tigers and bears, elephants and giraffe, flamingoes, rabbits and foxes, all climbed onto the ark that Noah had built.

And when the last one was on board, the rain began to fall.

Help me to trust you, Lord, step by step, even when I can't see how things will turn out in the end.

50

When disaster strikes

How do you feel when you can't see an end to something bad happening in your life?

When bad times come, and everything seems dull and difficult, give me hope, Lord. Help me to take each day as it comes and wait for you to bring light into the darkness.

 Genesis 7:11 – 8:7

Noah and his wife, his sons and their wives, fed the animals and cleared up after them. They heard the rain drumming on the roof, hour after hour, day after day, for forty days and forty nights. Streams became rivers and rivers became seas. The ark rose steadily on the floodwaters till there was nothing to be seen but water, water everywhere around them.

Then one day, they all looked at each other and listened. Silence. The rain had stopped. Noah watched as a strong wind blew the clouds away.

The ark came to rest on Mount Ararat and slowly, very slowly, the waters began to go down.

Are you surprised when God keeps his promises?

Noah trusted God to make things come right. The first thing he did afterwards was to thank him.

📖 *Genesis 8:15 – 9:17*

Noah and his family watched and waited a long time before the waters went down and the earth was dry again.

Finally God told Noah it was safe to open the door of the ark. Noah set all the animals free.

'Now they can increase and grow again in numbers,' said God.

Noah brought his family out of the ark and all the animals streamed out too, one kind after another, two by two. The earth was clean and new.

Noah made an altar to God and thanked him for keeping his family and all the animals safe from the flood. It was time to start again.

And God put a beautiful rainbow in the sky. 'Whenever you see a rainbow, remember my promise that the earth will never again be destroyed by flood.'

I am sorry, Lord, when I am ungrateful and forget to say thank you. I thank you now for keeping your promises. Thank you for answering my prayers. Thank you for…

When God wants you to act...

Abraham was not a young adventurer, keen to explore new places. But he trusted God with his future and when God said move, he moved.

📖 *Genesis 12:1-5*

Show me what you want me to do today and every day, Lord. And when you speak, help me to listen and to act.

Abraham was living in the land of Haran when God spoke to him.

'It's time to move on,' God said. 'Pack up all your things and take your family and servants with you. I will tell you where to go.'

Abraham and his wife Sarah were already old. They didn't know where they were going, and they didn't know how long it would take them, but they trusted God.

Abraham gathered up the tents where he lived, and all the things he owned and went with his wife, Sarah, his nephew, Lot, his servants, sheep, goats and cattle… far away from his home and across the hot, dusty desert.

They made camp many times on their long journey until they arrived in the land of Canaan. Then Abraham saw that the place that God had given them as their new home was beautiful.

God's plans for Abraham

How do we respond when God chooses to bless us?

📖 *Genesis 12:7, Deuteronomy 31:20*

The land of Canaan was made green by water. Everywhere trees and plants were growing. There would be plenty of food for Abraham's animals. It was a good place to be.

'Now I will bless you, Abraham,' God said. 'This land will belong to your children and your children's children.'

Abraham loved God and he trusted him but he couldn't help wondering how that could happen when he and Sarah didn't have even one tiny baby of their own.

I know I don't deserve your love, Lord. Thank you for all the blessings, all the good things you have given to me.

Do you find it hard to wait?

Abraham and Sarah lived each day knowing that God would bless them one day with what they wanted most of all.

 Genesis 13:5-13

Help us to be patient, Lord, and to make each day count even if we are waiting for you to answer our prayers.

Abraham and Sarah waited for God to give them a baby, but no baby came. Their lives were busy. Each day was full. Abraham's sheep had baby sheep, his goats had baby goats and God blessed Abraham and Lot so much that they couldn't move for animals!

'Choose anywhere you would like to live, Lot,' Abraham said to his nephew. 'We'll share the land between us so there is room for us all to be happy.' Lot chose the land to the east, a beautiful green valley, watered by the River Jordan near Sodom and Gomorrah. But Lot's neighbours were known for the bad, cruel things they did and they had no love for God.

God gives strength when we feel weak

The prophet Isaiah comforted God's people when they felt God had deserted them.

 Isaiah 40:27-31

How can you say that God doesn't see your troubles and isn't being fair? Don't you know that the everlasting God, the creator of the earth, never grows faint or weary? None of us can understand all that he knows – he is so much bigger than our imagination.

God gives power to those who are tired and worn out, he gives strength to the weak. Even the young become exhausted and eventually give up, but those who wait upon the Lord become strong once more. They are lifted up as if they have wings like eagles; they run without tiring and walk as if they could walk for ever.

Lord, when we feel weak and cannot go on, please lift us up and make us strong.

Help us to remember that sometimes the answer to our prayers is to wait and sometimes it may be no…

God keeps his promises

Sometimes God sends us answers in unexpected ways.

 Genesis 18:1-10

Abraham was resting in the shade in the heat of the day when he thought he saw three strangers walking towards him.

    Abraham got to his feet and went to greet them. He offered them somewhere to rest and started to prepare food for them to eat.

    As they spoke Abraham began to realize that God had sent them to him with a very special message.

    'Get ready for a wonderful surprise,' they said. 'By this time next year, Sarah will be nursing your baby son.'

    Sarah was listening from inside her tent. She laughed sadly to herself. Surely she was far too old to have a baby now?

Be welcoming to strangers

Abraham was welcoming to the men who visited him and found that God had sent them.

📖 Hebrews 13:1-3

Love each other as if you really mean it. Don't forget to be kind to strangers, for some who have done this have entertained angels without realizing it. Treat them as if they were your special guests.

Don't forget about people who are in prison. Try to understand how they feel and be kind to them.

If someone you know is being treated badly, let them tell you about it. Share their sadness.

Please Lord, help me to see everyone I meet as a person to respect and treat kindly.

How much do we care about justice?

Abraham asked God to be fair – and to show mercy to those who did not deserve it.

📖 *Genesis 18:17-33*

God had heard about the bad things that were happening in Sodom and Gomorrah. The strangers who had come to see Abraham went on to see if the people there were as bad as everyone believed. If they were, the cities would be destroyed.

Abraham knew that God was fair. So he asked, 'Will you spare the cities if only fifty good people live there?' God said, 'I will spare them.'

Abraham asked again, 'What if there are forty-five good people?' God said, 'I will spare them.'

Abraham kept asking until finally he said, 'Please, Lord, will you spare the cities if only ten good people live there?'

God promised that he would not destroy them for the sake of just ten good people.

Help us to pray for those things that really matter – and not give up.

How far would you go to protect someone in need?

Lot would not let any harm come to the strangers in his house.

📖 *Genesis 19:1-10*

The strangers sent by God to Sodom and Gomorrah were angels. Lot still lived there with his wife and daughters. He came to meet the strangers and welcomed them at the gate of the city.

'Come to my home and rest,' said Lot. 'Let me prepare food for you.'

But when the people of the city found out that Lot had strangers in his home, they hammered on his door. They demanded that Lot send them out. Lot stood in the doorway to protect his visitors but the men outside were fierce and angry. The angels pulled Lot back inside. There were only four good people left in the city.

Help us to stand up to bullies, Lord, and to be there for anyone who needs our help.

Mixing with the wrong crowd

Lot was loyal to God and kept his values even though they were very different from those of his neighbours.

Genesis 19:14-26

Lot was a good man. The angels warned him to take his family and any friends he had and run as far away as possible. The city would be destroyed by the morning.

But only his wife and daughters would go with Lot; only four people escaped that night.

'Don't look back!' the angels called after them. Lot and his family ran until they could run no more. They heard the terrible sound as fire and brimstone rained down on the cities of Sodom and Gomorrah.

Lot's wife looked back at the burning city – and was turned into a pillar of salt. Only Lot and his daughters were saved.

Help us to keep away from people who would lead us into harm's way and to stay loyal to you wherever we are.

Abraham's trust in God

Do you expect to have everything you want instantly? Abraham learned to wait for God's timing.

📖 *Genesis 21:1-8*

Abraham knew that God had answered his prayers about Sodom and Gomorrah and gone even further, because he had saved the good people left in the city.

Soon Abraham also knew that God had kept his promise about a baby for Sarah. Abraham was going to be a father at last. It was a miracle.

Abraham was as impatient as Sarah to hold his little baby son in his arms.

'God has made me so happy!' said Sarah when her son was born.

They named their baby Isaac, which means laughter, because Sarah had laughed when she was told she would have a baby.

Teach us patience, Lord. Help us to wait for our prayers to be answered.

What would you give up for God?

Abraham put no limits on what he would do if God asked him.

 Genesis 22:1-8

Abraham loved and trusted God and couldn't thank him enough for his precious son.

So when God asked Abraham to do something very hard indeed, Abraham was very sad. Isaac had grown into a fine boy. Now God was asking Abraham to trust him with the son he loved more than anything. Abraham took Isaac with him up the mountain with a heavy heart.

'We have the wood for the sacrifice, but where is the lamb?' asked Isaac.

'Don't worry,' said Abraham. 'God will provide the sacrifice.'

We want to be willing to do anything you ask, Lord. Please help...

Abraham's faith

God doesn't test us more than we can take… but Abraham must have loved God very much.

📖 *Genesis 22:9-18*

Abraham took the knife in his hand ready to give Isaac back to God – but before he had time to use it, an angel stopped him.

Abraham put down the knife and hugged his son very, very tightly.

'Now I know how much you love me,' said God. 'I know you trust me even when it is very hard. I will bless you, now and always.'

Then Abraham saw a ram caught in a bush. He sacrificed the animal instead.

Help us to love you as much as Abraham, Lord, so we can trust you with the difficult things in our lives.

When you need guidance...

Abraham's servant knew he needed God's help to make the right choice.

 Genesis 24:1-14

Isaac was a man by the time his mother died. Abraham wanted to find for him a wife from his own family rather than from the people who lived nearby. So Abraham sent his servant on a long journey to find a good, kind woman who would be happy to be Isaac's wife.

When the servant arrived at the place where Abraham's family still lived, he was tired and very thirsty. He sat down and prayed for God's help.

'Please help me to find a girl for Isaac – someone kind enough to offer me water to drink on this hot day – and then water my ten camels too.'

Please show us how to make the right choices in life. Please guide us today.

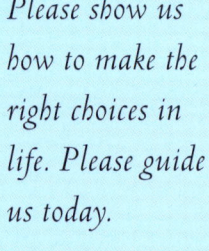

Do we thank God for answered prayers?

Abraham's servant thanked God for helping him make the right choice.

📖 *Genesis 24:15-24*

Abraham's servant saw many girls coming to draw water from the well. One was very beautiful.

'May I have a drink?' the servant asked her.

'Of course!' she answered. She drew the water from the well and offered it to him. Then the girl added, 'Let me bring some water for your camels too. They must be so thirsty!'

He discovered that the girl was called Rebekah and that she was the granddaughter of Abraham's brother. He had come to the right place.

The servant silently thanked God. He knew that God had answered his prayer and that he would be able to take back the right wife for Isaac.

Thank you, Lord, for the prayers you have answered for me.

Parents aren't perfect...

Isaac and Rebekah were blessed with two children but they each had a favourite.

 Genesis 25:20-29

Isaac and Rebekah were married and were together for some years before Rebekah told him he would be a father – and then it was with twins.

Esau was born first, strong and healthy with lots of red hair. He grew up to be a skilful hunter and loved the outdoor life. Isaac was proud of his eldest son. He liked spending time with Esau best of all.

Jacob was born second, dark in colouring with smooth skin. Jacob was a quiet boy, Rebekah's favourite. Esau would often come back from a day's hunting to smell something good simmering in a pot that Jacob had cooked.

Please bless our family, Lord, to love each other and take care of each other.

How to be a happy family

The apostle Paul knew that family life could be difficult and gave this advice.

📖 *Ephesians 6:1-4*

'Children, obey your parents – it's the right thing to do. God has given them to you to take care of you and they usually know best. Listen to them and respect them as God's commandments tell you to.

    'Parents, try to be positive. Don't keep on scolding and nagging your children because it will make them angry and resentful. Love them but also discipline them so they know how important right is from wrong. Find ways to teach them this so they see the wisdom of loving God and doing the right thing.'

Help us to say 'I love you' lots. Help us to say 'thank you' and 'I'm sorry' often.

God's family

The apostle Paul reminds us that we are different once we have become Christians.

 Colossians 3:9-11

Help us to treat the other people in our church as part of our wider family and take care of them.

'If you love God, you won't tell lies to each other – that's what people do when they don't know God; and you are different.

'Every day God is making you more like Jesus and you will want to do what is right. It doesn't matter where you come from or what school you went to. It doesn't matter whether you are black or white, rich or poor. The only thing that is important is whether we belong to Christ because that makes us family. And anyone and everyone is welcome in that family.'

The importance of love

Do others see Jesus in the way we speak and act towards them?

📖 *Colossians 3:12-17*

'God loves you and cares about you,' said the apostle Paul, 'and the way you show how much that matters is that you should love and care about others. Be kind, be ready to forgive and never hold grudges. Just as God forgives you for the bad things you do, so you must forgive others.

'Let love guide your life. With love in your dealings towards everyone, peace and harmony will follow.

'Remember what Jesus taught and share his words with each other. Thank God for the good things he has done for you. And remember that whatever you do or say, it reflects upon Jesus.'

May everything we do today be kind, generous, thoughtful and unselfish.

Is your family perfect?

No one is perfect, so it's not surprising that things go wrong in families.

Help us not to let small problems become bigger problems in our family but to talk things through together.

 Genesis 25:29-34

Esau returned to his father's tents one day hot and tired and hungry. He followed the spicy smell to Jacob and the lentil stew he was cooking.

'Mmmm, that smells delicious,' Esau said. 'I'm so hungry, I could die!'

Jacob was quiet but he was clever. He kept stirring the stew.

'You can have some now,' he replied, 'as long as you will trade it for father's blessing.'

They both knew that only the older son was allowed that special blessing given before their father died. Jacob had never felt that was fair.

'You can have anything you like if I can eat that stew!' replied Esau.

So Esau sold his birthright to Jacob and didn't seem to care.

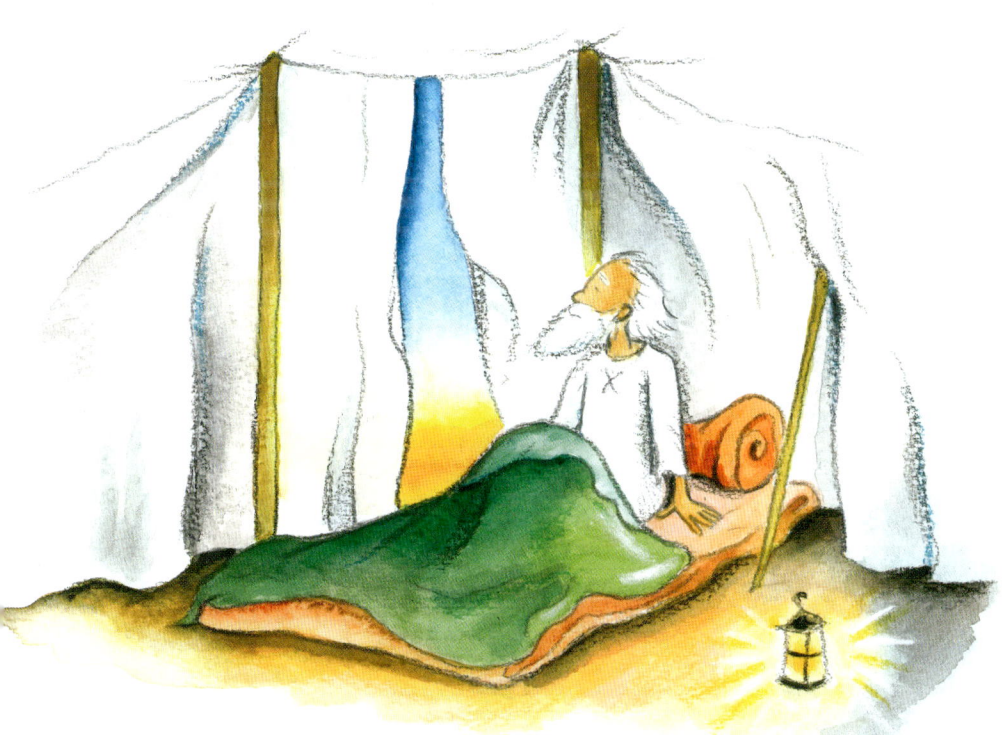

Parents and children

Is it a problem when parents have favourites?

 Genesis 27:1-5

Isaac grew to be an old man. His back became stooped. His eyes became dim. He soon found that he couldn't see very well at all. He called Esau to his tent one day.

'My son, I know it will not be long before I die. I want to give you my blessing. But first – go and hunt for me with your bow and arrow. Bring home something tasty and cook me my favourite meal.'

Isaac didn't know anything about Esau's trade with his younger brother years before. But Rebekah was listening. She had a plan.

Help us to be honest with each other in our family and to be fair in all we do.

Have you ever told a lie?

One bad decision often leads to many more; trouble leads to more trouble.

📖 *Genesis 27:5-17*

Jacob was Rebekah's favourite son; she wanted Jacob to have his father's blessing instead of Esau.

So while Esau was out hunting, Rebekah started to cook a tasty meal for Isaac. She called Jacob and told him to dress in some of Esau's clothes so that he would smell like his brother. Then Rebekah covered Jacob's neck and arms in goatskin so he would feel hairy like his brother.

Now everything was ready: Jacob could go to see his father and make him believe that he was blessing Esau. . .

Lord, help us to be open and honest in everything we do so that one small sin doesn't get us into lots more trouble.

Have you ever stolen anything?

Jacob lied to his father and then stole his brother's blessing...

 Genesis 27:18-29

Isaac heard someone come into his tent.

'Is that you already, Esau?' he asked his younger son. 'God must have blessed you to have such a good day's hunting.'

Then Isaac touched his son and felt his hairy skin; he smelled the clothes that he wore. Isaac was satisfied. He ate the meal that Rebekah had made for him and blessed Jacob.

'May God bless you now and always. You will become a rich man and will rule over your brother.'

Jacob had what he had always wanted – but he had done it by cheating and stealing.

For when we lie to others, forgive us, Lord. For when we steal from others, forgive us, Lord.

What should we do when our relationships are spoiled?

To know forgiveness we need to be sorry – and mean it.

 *Genesis 27:30-45*

Not long afterwards, Esau returned from his hunting trip. He prepared the food to take to his father and carried it into his tent.

'I have brought you your favourite meal, Father,' he said. 'I have come for your blessing.'

Then Isaac felt the pain of knowing that he had been tricked and Esau realized that he was too late for his father's blessing. They were both very angry.

'I'm going to kill my little brother for this!' Esau said. He went looking for Jacob.

Rebekah saw that the two brothers could not live together happily now.

'Go, Jacob,' she said to her youngest son. 'Go and stay with your Uncle Laban for a while. You will be safe there.'

Help us, Lord, to be quick to say sorry when we are in the wrong so that our love for each other is not spoiled for ever.

God's incredible love

Jacob, like us, did not deserve God's blessing – but God is more generous than we can ever know.

📖 *Genesis 28:10-15*

Jacob left his family and travelled till sunset when he lay down to sleep. Then Jacob dreamed…

In his dream Jacob saw a stairway which stretched from earth to heaven, and on it were angels climbing up and down. At the top was God himself!

'I am the Lord,' God said, 'the God of your father and your grandfather. I will give this place to your children and your grandchildren's children. There will be so many of them that they will spread all over this land. I am with you now and will watch over you and take care of you wherever you go; I will always be with you and bring you back here to your home.'

Thank you, Lord, that you do not wait for us to be perfect before you bless us; and that you are always more generous to us than we deserve.

76 Can we say that the living God is also our God?

Jacob realized that God was not only real but wanted to know him and take care of him.

Lord, come to me now so that you can be my God too, not just the God of the family you have given to me.

📖 *Genesis 28:18-22*

When Jacob woke up he was amazed at the promise God had made to him in his dream.

He took the stone he had rested his head on and set up a pillar as a memorial of what had happened in that place. He called it Bethel, which means the house of God; and Jacob made a promise to God, that from now on, the God of Abraham and of Isaac would also be his God, and he would give back to him a tenth of all that God gave him throughout his life, to show he was grateful for all the blessings he received.

God is good!

Can you remember some of the good things God has done for you?

 Psalm 27:1-13

The Lord leads me and saves me and makes me strong. Why should I be afraid of anyone?

I want to live in God's house for ever, to know that he is always there with me. I will give back my love to God with a thankful heart and will sing praises to him with joy in my heart.

Show your kindness to me, Lord, and be my helper now as you have before. I know you will take care of me.

Teach me your way, Lord, and lead me on the right path. I know I can trust you – I know your goodness will follow me throughout my life.

Thank you for all the good things you give to me, Lord. Thank you for…

The strength of love

What would you be prepared to do for someone you love?

 Genesis 29:1-18

Teach us, Lord, that things that matter most are worth waiting for and worth working for.

Jacob stopped by a well on the way to Haran where his uncle lived. There he met a beautiful shepherdess called Rachel; he knew straight away that he wanted to marry her. Then Jacob found out that the beautiful girl was his cousin. Rachel took Jacob to meet her father.

Soon Jacob was being welcomed into his uncle Laban's family and started to work for him, taking care of his sheep and goats.

After some time, Laban asked Jacob: 'You have worked hard for me. How can I reward you for all you have done?'

Jacob knew immediately what his answer would be. 'I will work for you for seven years if you will let me marry Rachel.'

How do you deal with big disappointments?

Things go wrong even for people who love God. But God does not leave us…

 Genesis 29:19-26

Laban had two daughters. Leah, who was older, was not yet married but Laban agreed to the marriage of his younger daughter. He knew that Jacob was strong and he could see that God had blessed him.

Jacob was happy to work hard for his uncle. Every day brought him nearer to the time when he could marry Rachel.

Seven years later, Jacob was married. But when he lifted the veil to kiss his new wife, he found that his uncle Laban had tricked him!

'It's our custom that the older sister is married first,' Laban explained.

Jacob had married not Rachel – but Leah! Jacob had been tricked. His uncle was not an honest man.

Be with us and help us, Lord, when bad things happen to us that are not our fault.

The ups and downs of life

Do we accept everything God gives – even if it doesn't seem like a blessing at first?

📖 *Genesis 29:27 – 30:24*

Thank you, Lord, for all the good things you give us. Help us to look for the blessing even in things we don't expect.

Jacob was very sad that Rachel was not his wife and he was angry that he had been tricked. But Laban told Jacob that as long as he worked for him for another seven years, he could marry Rachel as well as Leah. So, since many people had more than one wife at that time, Jacob married Rachel.

Rachel was very happy to be Jacob's wife at last, but Leah was not quite so happy. She knew that Jacob did not love her as much as he loved Rachel. So God blessed Leah with many children to love.

It was a long time before Rachel had a child and that made her sad. Jacob had ten sons and a daughter before Rachel gave birth to little Joseph.

Could people describe us as selfish?

Laban did not think of what was good for Jacob and his family but only what was good for him.

📖 *Genesis 30:25-43, 31:17-21*

When Jacob had been living with his uncle for a long time, he decided he wanted to go home.

Laban was a selfish man; he knew that God had blessed him while Jacob had been there and he didn't want that to change.

'Wait till you have built up a herd of speckled or spotted animals,' Laban suggested.

Then Laban hid the animals so Jacob could not breed from them! Laban was still a man who could not be trusted.

But Jacob found a way to breed the sheep and goats secretly so that soon, everywhere he looked, the animals were black and white and every variation of spotted and speckled! When his herd was big and strong, Jacob gathered his wives and children and all his animals – and crept away, without telling his uncle.

Lord, make us people who think more about the needs of others than of ourselves.

82

I don't want to bear grudges or be the one who turns my back on others, Lord. Help me please to put things right.

Are there broken relationships in your life you have never fixed?

Whether it's our fault or the other person's, God can help us be the first to say sorry.

📖 *Genesis 32:24-28*

Jacob knew that God had kept his promises and had blessed him with a large family and more than he could have imagined. But he also knew that he had made his brother angry and was worried about what would happen when he met Esau again.

One night, he was sitting alone by a river when a stranger came and wrestled with him. When the sun rose, Jacob realized that the stranger had not been a man but an angel sent by God.

'From now on your name will be Israel,' said the angel. 'God has special plans for you.'

After this, Jacob's children and his children's children came to be known as the Israelites.

Do you get angry easily?

The apostle Paul said that people who know Jesus throw off their own nature and are clothed in a new one.

📖 *Ephesians 4:2, 21-26, 31-32*

'If you have really heard the call of Jesus, throw off the way you used to behave as you would an old dirty, coat. What you think and the way you behave must always be changing for the better. You must be a new person, a good person. Put on this new nature as if putting on a new piece of clothing.

'Stop lying and tell the truth. If you are angry, don't nurse a grudge or go to bed before putting it right. Stop being unkind or bad-tempered or angry. Don't use bad words to each other but instead be gentle and forgiving to one another, in the same way that God has forgiven you.'

Don't let me hold on to the bad ways I knew before I loved you, Lord. Change me to be a better person.

84

We gain nothing by worrying…

Nothing changes for the better when we are nervous or anxious – and things often turn out better when we trust God.

 Genesis 33:1-4

The day had come when Jacob was to meet his brother again. Many years had passed. Jacob was nervous – and became very worried when he saw that Esau had come out to meet him with 400 men!

Jacob told his family to wait in safety while he went on alone to meet Esau and his army.

Jacob could hardly believe his eyes when he saw that Esau was smiling and coming forward to hug him.

Esau had forgiven Jacob long ago. Now they were not just brothers but friends. God really had blessed Jacob.

Thank you, God, that you bring good things out of bad, again and again and again…

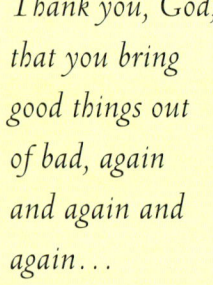

The blessings and the bad stuff

All our lives are made up of blessings and terrible sadnesses. God is there through them all.

 Genesis 35:9-20, 16-19, 27-29

God blessed Jacob again after his meeting with Esau. 'Your name is Jacob, but you will now be known as Israel. I am your God: this land will be your land, just as I gave it to Abraham and to Isaac.'

Jacob marked the place where God had blessed him and called it Bethel.

Before they reached Bethlehem, Rachel went into labour with her second son. But Rachel had a difficult time; just after baby Benjamin was born, Rachel died. She was buried on the way to Bethlehem and Jacob marked the place where he left his much-loved wife.

Then Jacob went home to see his father Isaac, who was now a very old man. When Isaac died, he was buried by his two sons.

Lord, help us when we meet great sadness and lose those we love.

The blessings of God

Are we willing to accept only the good things that God gives us?

📖 Job 1 – 2

Job was a good man. God had blessed him with a big family, good health and many riches. Then one day, he lost everything. Four disasters happened so that he lost all his wealth and his ten children were killed.

Job fell on his knees and cried out to God. 'I brought nothing into this world at my birth and I will take nothing with me when I die. The Lord blessed me with many good things and now he has taken them away. I will praise him because he is my God.'

The following day Job became very ill and was covered in painful sores. His friends could barely recognize him.

'How can you still trust God?' his wife said.

'Don't be silly,' said Job. 'Should we only accept the good that God gives us and not the bad?'

Help us to trust you even when everything goes wrong, Lord, even when we are in pain.

God is beyond understanding

Job never found out why he had suffered so much but he trusted God through good and bad.

87

 *Job 4 – 42*

Job was suffering deeply but he still trusted God. Yet he did want to know what he had done to deserve such suffering. After he had talked long and hard with God, God answered him.

'Why do you talk so much when you know so little? Were you there when I laid the foundations of the earth? Have you walked on the ocean floor or arranged the stars in the night skies?

'Did you teach the birds how to know if storms are approaching? Did you give horses their strength or teach the hawks to fly south for the winter? Did you train the eagles to build nests on rocky cliffs?'

Job realized how little he knew of God. But God also saw that Job had continued to love him even in his suffering. God made him even more wealthy than before and gave him seven more sons and three more daughters. Job died when he was very old.

Lord, you alone are God and in you we put our trust.

Have you ever wanted to run away from God?

The prophet Jonah did. He didn't find it easy to do the things God told him to do.

 Jonah 1:1-3

Jonah was one of God's prophets. When he heard God speak, he took the message to the people.

'Go to Nineveh,' said God. 'I have seen the terrible things the Assyrians are doing. Tell them to stop – or I will punish them.'

Jonah knew about the cruel Assyrians and he believed they deserved God's punishment. But Jonah knew God was loving and forgiving – and he didn't want to go. Let those wicked people suffer!

So Jonah went down to the port at Joppa and boarded a ship heading for Tarshish – about as far in the opposite direction as he could go. He paid his fare, found somewhere below deck to hide away – and fell asleep.

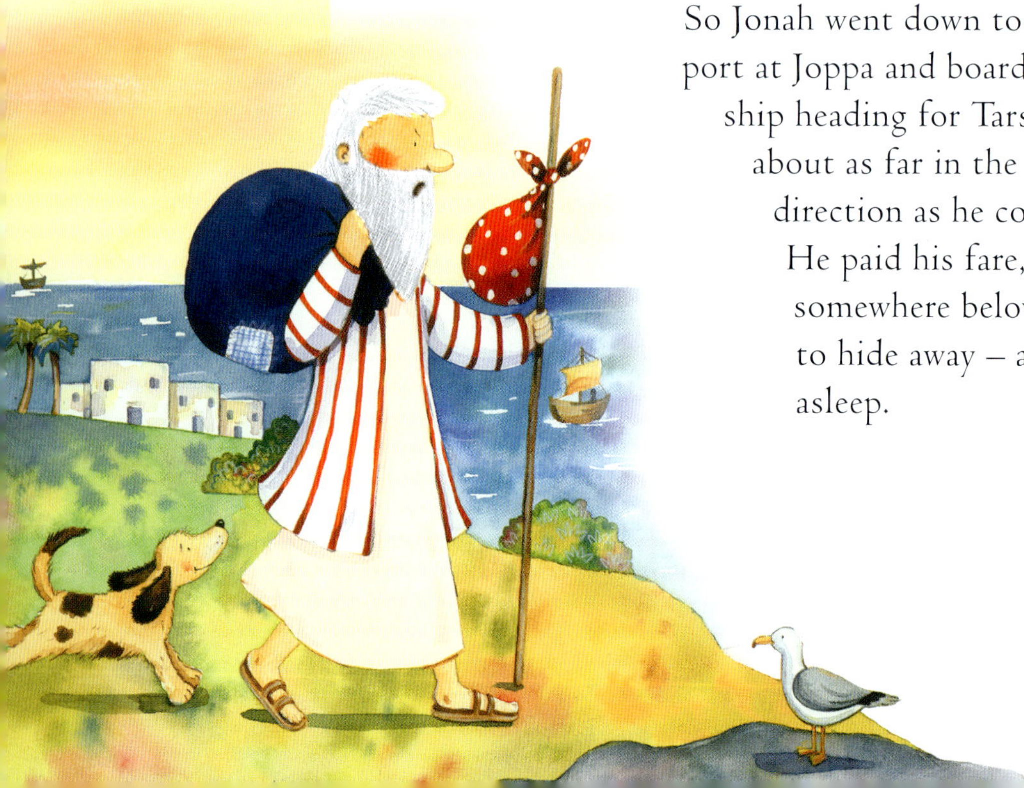

Lord, sometimes I don't want to listen when you speak. Help me when I want to close my ears and do what I want to do instead of the right thing.

Prophets aren't perfect

God chooses ordinary people to serve him. Like us, they don't always get it right.

📖 *Jonah 1:4-6*

While Jonah was sleeping on the ship, a great wind blew and tore at the ship's sails. Huge rolling waves rocked it up and down dangerously and water sloshed over the sides.

The ship sailing for Tarshish suddenly found itself in the middle of a violent storm. The sailors were so afraid, they threw the cargo overboard to save themselves. They woke the sleeping Jonah.

'Who are you and where do you come from?' they shouted. 'Pray to your God for help!'

Then Jonah knew what had happened. 'I am a Hebrew and I worship the living God who made the land and sea,' he told them. 'But I have run away because I didn't want to obey him. This is all my fault.'

Lord, when I make mistakes, help me to admit it and face up to what I need to do to put things right.

Putting others first

Jonah didn't know what God would do next but he stopped thinking about himself and thought about the sailors who were going to die.

 Jonah 1:9-12

The waves were whooshing higher and higher and the wind was howling. The sailors were now terrified.

'What shall we do?' they shouted, clinging on for their lives. Jonah knew the answer.

'Pick me up and throw me over the side,' he shouted back. 'Then the sea will be calm again and you will be safe.'

The sailors didn't want to hurt Jonah so they tried to row back to land – but the sea grew wilder. They realized there was no other way.

So the sailors threw Jonah overboard, down into the deep blue sea.

Would I be brave enough to die if I could save someone else? Help me, Lord, to start by putting other people first today.

In God's safe hands

Our faith matters most when it is tested; and Jonah put himself in God's hands as he fell into the sea.

 *Jonah 1:15-17*

Jonah fell down, down, down into the cold, salty sea and straight away, God stilled the raging storm.

    The sailors on the ship saw that Jonah's God was very great because he could still a storm as easily as he could make it rage and roar. They fell to their knees in awe of him.

    Then God sent a great sea creature through the water to swallow Jonah whole.

    The prophet sat in the belly of the creature for three days and three nights. Jonah knew that God had saved him.

Lord, let me not be a fair-weather Christian who trusts you only when things go right. Help me to trust you in the darkest moments of my life.

Do we pray only when things go wrong?

Jonah called out to God for help but he also thanked him and worshipped God when he prayed.

📖 *Jonah 2:1-10*

Jonah sat inside the body of the sea creature and he prayed.

'I was in great trouble and you were there for me, Lord! You heard me even from the depths of the sea. I thought I was dying but you rescued me. When I was surrounded by water and seaweed was wrapped around my head, you saved me.

'I had almost given up hope but when I called you answered. Thank you for giving me another chance. I will worship no one else but you for I can never thank you enough for what you have done for me! I promised to serve you and I will serve you because only you have the power to save!'

Then God told the creature to spit Jonah out on to dry land.

Lord, help me to talk to you when things go right, not just when they go wrong. Help me to praise you and worship you, not just ask for things.

What makes us afraid to tell people about God?

Often people are waiting for us to share what we know about God with them.

 Jonah 3:1-4

Now Jonah was back on dry land. This time when God told him to go to Nineveh with his warning for the people, Jonah went.

As he approached the great city, Jonah shouted out, 'Listen to what God says: in forty days Nineveh will be destroyed!'

It took three days for Jonah to reach all the people with the message, from the shopkeepers and soldiers to the king in his palace. The cruel people of Nineveh did not attack Jonah; they did not ignore him or laugh at him. Instead they stopped and listened and took what he said very seriously. They stopped feasting and partying; they stopped bullying and fighting; and instead they started to pray.

Lord, help me to share what I know about you with others today.

What being sorry means

The people of Nineveh did what we should all do when we say we are sorry – they changed their ways.

📖 *Jonah 3:5-10*

The people of Nineveh realized they had done things which were wrong – and they were sorry. They showed how sorry they were by taking off their beautiful clothes and putting on rough, coarse clothes called sackcloth which were usually worn when someone had died.

The people of Nineveh begged God for forgiveness. Even the king tore off his beautiful robes and wore itchy sackcloth to show God that he was sorry. He told the people to turn away from the cruel and violent things they were doing in the hope that God might forgive them.

God saw that the people had changed their ways. He did forgive them and had compassion for them.

Lord, thank you that you forgive all those who come to you and say sorry.

Have you ever wanted to get someone into trouble?

Jonah should have been happy that the God he worshipped was kind and compassionate and forgiving. But Jonah wasn't.

📖 Jonah 4:1-11

Jonah was angry with God. Surely the people were wicked? Wicked people deserved to be punished – they deserved to die. Jonah went away and sulked.

But God said, 'Jonah, is it right to be angry about this?'

As Jonah sat in the hot sun, God caused a vine to grow up and give him shade. But then a worm ate the plant so it died – and Jonah was very unhappy.

'Look Jonah – I gave you a vine to shelter under when you needed shade. You didn't make the vine or take care of it but when it withered and died you were unhappy. Can't you understand therefore how I care about these people? I made them; I love them; and I care what happens to them.'

Lord, teach me to be as kind and forgiving as you are. Forgive me when I bear grudges against people.

Do you ever wish that you were someone else?

Each of us is special, with different gifts and personalities – even if others don't always appreciate it.

 Genesis 37:3-8

Help me to accept who I am, Lord, and to be happy to be me – and not someone else.

Joseph, Rachel's first-born son, knew that he was his father's favourite. So did all his brothers…

One day Jacob, Joseph's father, made a present of a beautiful long sleeved coat to Joseph. It made Joseph feel very special – but his brothers looked at each other. Were they not special too? It was hard to know that your father did not treat his children fairly.

One night, Joseph dreamed a very strange dream. He told his family about it the next morning.

'Listen,' he said. 'I dreamed that we were all tying bundles of grain. Then my bundle stood up very straight while yours all bowed down in front of mine!'

The brothers looked angry. Did it mean something? Would Joseph one day rule over his older brothers like a king?

Could you hate someone enough to wish them harm?

Jesus said that if we hate someone in our hearts it's as bad as committing murder.

📖 *Genesis 37:11-24*

Joseph's brothers often looked after their father's sheep far from home. One day, Jacob sent Joseph to see how they were. They saw him when he was still a long way off.

'Look who's coming!' they said to each other. 'Here comes that dreamer!'

They were not just jealous of Joseph – by now they hated him!

'Let's kill him!' said one. 'We could tell our father that he has been eaten by a wild animal!'

When everyone agreed, Reuben, the oldest brother, stopped them. 'Let's throw him into this dry well for a while so we can think about what to do,' he suggested. Reuben secretly planned to rescue him later.

So when Joseph came to greet them, his brothers tore off his special coat and put him in a deep, dark hole…

I want to pray for the people I know whom I cannot love, the people who I really don't like at all…

How well do you know yourself?

Sometimes it takes a bad thing to happen before we see ourselves as others see us.

 *Genesis 37:25-34*

Lord, help me not to think so much of myself that I don't realize when what I say or do hurts or upsets others.

The brothers settled down to eat their lunch while Joseph, confused and frightened, shouted for help from the deep hole in the ground.

What was happening to him? Why were his brothers treating him this way?

Then some spice traders on camels passed by. The brothers struck a deal with them. They hauled Joseph out of the pit and sold him for twenty silver coins.

Now Joseph was on his way to Egypt where he would be sold to be a slave. When the brothers returned to their father, they told him a sad story of how a wild animal had attacked Joseph and killed him.

Jacob felt as if the world had ended. He had lost his favourite son.

Do you fall apart when things go wrong or try to make the best of it?

God promises to give us strength even when things don't seem to be working out.

📖 *Genesis 39:1-20*

On the long, dusty journey, Joseph began to realize that his brothers must hate him.

But God had not forgotten Joseph. When he reached Egypt, he was sold as a slave to Potiphar, who was a kind master. Joseph did his best and worked very hard. He proved to be good at everything he did so that soon, Potiphar trusted Joseph with everything in his house. God blessed Potiphar because Joseph was there.

Not everything went well, however. Joseph was a handsome young man and Potiphar's wife liked him very much – too much, in fact. Every day she would try to kiss him – and every day, Joseph would try to get away from her!

One day Potiphar's wife was so angry with Joseph that she told her husband lies about him – and Potiphar sent Joseph to prison.

Lord, help me to do the best I can in whatever situation, good or bad.

The right place and the right time

Sometimes miracles are not impossible things but the fact they happen when and where they do.

📖 *Genesis 39:21 – 40:19*

Joseph worked hard in the prison and God blessed him again. The guard trusted him and soon Joseph was his helper.

One day, the king's baker and butler were thrown into prison too. Joseph listened as they told him about the dreams they had dreamed the night before. The baker dreamed he had made three loaves of bread for the king, but the birds came along and ate them all.

The butler dreamed that the king drank wine he had made from three branches of grapes.

'What can it mean?' they asked.

God helped Joseph to understand both dreams.

'Don't worry!' Joseph told the butler. 'In three days, you will be working once more for the king!' But there was bad news for the baker. 'I'm sorry, but in three days, you will be hanged. . .'

Help me to make the best of all the opportunities you give me, Lord, and to watch and listen for when I could be useful.

Watching and waiting

God works out his purposes in his time, not ours.

📖 *Genesis 40:20 – 41:13*

Joseph had been right about the dreams. 'Tell the king I did nothing wrong!' he said to the butler when he left the prison.

Two years later the king had strange dreams. Seven fat, healthy cows were grazing by the Nile when seven skinny, bony cows came up and ate them. Then seven thin parched ears of grain swallowed up seven plump golden ears of grain.

The king was very worried.

'What can it mean?' he asked all the wise men in his court. But no one could tell the king the meaning of his dream.

Then the butler dared to speak. 'When I was in prison I met a man, an innocent man, who knows how to understand the meaning of dreams. Perhaps he can help you?'

Teach me patience, Lord, and help me to learn from even things that seem to me to be wasted time.

Our place in the puzzle

Although we can't see the greater plan when we are in it, God uses us to make good things happen.

📖 *Genesis 41:14-36*

Thank you, Lord, for using me, even me, to do good things.

Joseph had almost given up hope of being free when he was brought from the prison, washed and shaved, and made to kneel before the great king of Egypt.

When the king told Joseph his strange dreams, Joseph answered, 'I cannot explain your dreams, oh king, but my God knows everything. Your dreams both give the same warning. Soon we will have seven years of wonderful harvests followed by seven years when nothing grows at all. There will be a terrible famine. What you need is someone to store all the grain in the first seven years so that no one will go hungry when the famine comes.'

Are we changed for the better by difficult situations?

Joseph had been changed from a spoilt child into a responsible man.

 *Genesis 41:37-57*

The king smiled at Joseph and called him forward.

'Surely you are the man to take charge!' he said. 'God has told you what will happen – everyone will take orders from you.'

Then the great king of Egypt placed a ring on Joseph's hand, gave him fine clothes to wear and put a gold chain around his neck. He gave him a chariot to ride in wherever he went.

The good harvests came to Egypt, followed by the famine, just as Joseph had said. The people of Egypt cried out to the king for help in their hunger, and Joseph opened the storehouses of grain and made sure everyone had enough to eat.

Joseph had become the most important man in Egypt apart from the king himself.

Lord, change me into what you want me to be.

Do you believe God has plans for your life?

God's plans for Joseph took many years to unfold but now he was in the right place to help his family.

📖 *Genesis 42:1-8*

104

Help me, Lord, to trust you for each step of the way on my faith journey.

Famine spread across the whole region. Joseph's family in Canaan was also affected. So Jacob sent his older sons to Egypt to buy food for them all. Only Benjamin, Jacob's youngest son, stayed at home with his father.

When Joseph's brothers bowed low before the man who was the second most powerful in all the land of Egypt, they did not recognize the boy who had told them of his strange dreams.

But Joseph recognized his brothers.

'We are your humble servants,' they said. 'We are hungry and have come to buy food.'

Were Joseph's brothers the same men who had wanted to kill him? Were they sorry that they had sold him to be a slave for twenty silver coins?

Are you ever tempted to take revenge on those who hurt you?

Joseph must have lost hope many times – but he began to see the part he was playing in God's plan.

📖 *Genesis 42:9-17*

105

Even when things don't work out for me, Lord, help me to learn from the experience.

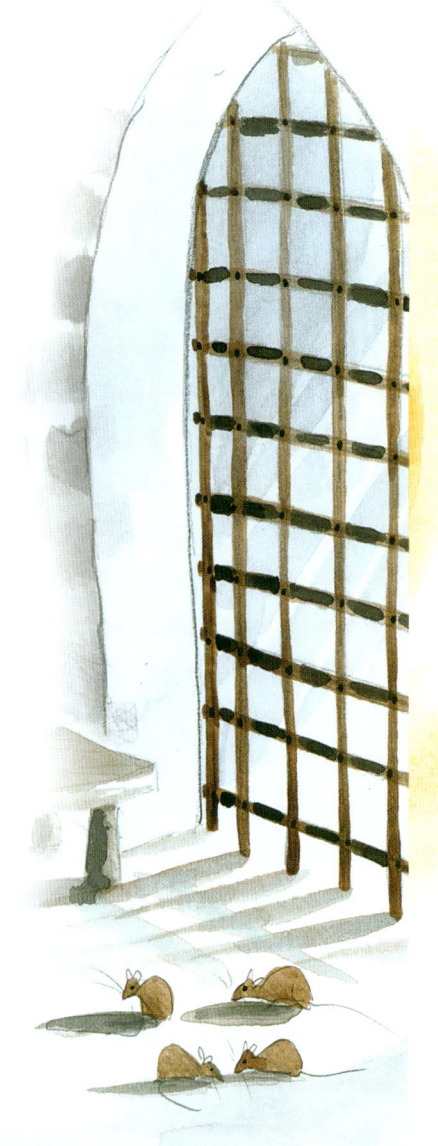

Joseph decided to test his brothers. He pretended he did not understand them and used an interpreter.

'Where do you come from? Surely you are here to spy on us!'

'No,' they replied. 'We are honest, the sons of one man. We were twelve brothers, but the youngest is still with our father in Canaan, and one has already died.'

'No, I don't trust you!' said Joseph. 'Prove you are honest men! You must bring your youngest brother here to me so I know you are telling the truth!'

Then Joseph put them all in prison for three days to think about what he had said.

Do you know what it is like to feel guilty?

Living with guilt is a painful process; admitting our fault and asking to be forgiven sets us free.

 Genesis 42:18-26

When Joseph released his brothers, he was kinder.

'I, too, believe in God,' he said. 'I want one man to stay here as a hostage while the rest of you return with food for your family. Then you must come back here with your youngest brother.'

Then the brothers spoke to each other believing that Joseph could not understand them.

'This is all our fault! We are being punished because of what we did to Joseph – we wouldn't listen when he pleaded with us not to hurt him. What we did was wrong!'

Joseph was very upset at what he heard but he hid his feelings. Instead he had Simeon tied up and taken from them while the others were given food for the journey and sacks of grain to take home. Then he secretly returned the money they had paid to their bags.

Lord, make me honest, with you and with others. Forgive me for the bad things and set me free from the guilt I feel.

Do we doubt that God is taking care of us?

Jacob could only see the bad things that were happening now, not the good things to come.

📖 *Genesis 42:27-38*

When Joseph's brothers found that their money had been returned, they were very afraid. How could they go back to Egypt now? It would look as though they had stolen the food.

They told Jacob all that had happened and explained that if they were to see Simeon again, they must take Benjamin to Egypt.

Jacob did not know what to do.

'How can I do this? Do you want me to lose all my children?! Joseph is gone and now Simeon is gone – and yet you want me to lose Benjamin too! Everything is against me!'

Then Reuben offered his own precious children to his father. 'Trust me with Benjamin – we will come back and all will be well.'

Jacob was still not happy. 'I will die if anything happens to Benjamin!' he said.

When things go wrong, please help me to remember your promises and trust you for the good things around the corner.

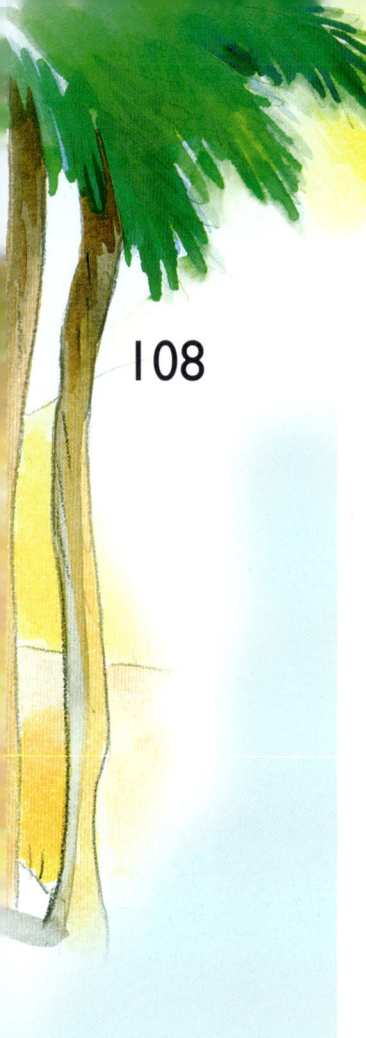

How far would you go to protect someone you love?

Joseph's brothers had hurt their father once before – they would not do it again.

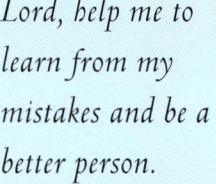 *Genesis 44:1-34*

When Benjamin arrived with his brothers, Joseph was overjoyed to see him! But he still kept secret who he really was. He had another test for them.

This time, when the brothers were ready to return to Canaan, Joseph put a silver cup into Benjamin's sack of grain so it looked as if he were a thief!

Would his brothers defend Benjamin? Or would they leave him behind?

Joseph's servant shouted, 'STOP! Someone has stolen my master's silver cup!'

Ten sacks were all searched and nothing was found. Then they looked in Benjamin's sack – and there was the missing cup! The brothers wept.

'Please! Punish me, not Benjamin!' they said. 'It will break our father's heart if he does not return!'

Lord, help me to learn from my mistakes and be a better person.

Do you remember still someone who has hurt you in some way?

Learning to forgive is good for you and for the person you have forgiven.

📖 *Genesis 45:1-24*

Joseph now knew that his brothers were not the same men who had sold him as a slave. They were sorry for what they had done and were now kinder men. Joseph forgave them for all the bad things that had happened.

'Look!' he told them. 'I am Joseph, your brother. You meant to harm me, but it was God's plan all along to bring me to Egypt. I have been able to help our family not to die of hunger.'

Then Joseph hugged his brothers. There were friends for the first time.

The king told Joseph to let his brothers return with as much food as they could carry, then to invite the whole family to return to live in Egypt.

Take away my anger and my pain, Lord. Let me forgive as I have been forgiven.

God knows our weaknesses

God understood that Jacob would be afraid to leave Canaan and reassured him.

 Genesis 46:1-7, 28-30

When Jacob learned that Joseph was still alive – and that he could see him again, he cried with joy.

'Don't be afraid to make your home in Egypt,' God said to him. 'I will go there with you and I will bring you back. Joseph will be there with you when you die.'

Jacob took with him all his sons and their wives and children, all the aunts and uncles and cousins... There were hundreds of people.

When he met Joseph again they threw their arms around each other and cried. Now they were all together again – one big happy family.

They lived together in Egypt in a place called Goshen.

Thank you, Lord, that you know me better than I know myself and understand my fears.

Families matter

Whether we have a large family or a very small one, we matter to each other and should take care of each other.

 Genesis 50:1-26

Jacob died when he was a very old man.

Joseph was very, very sad when his father died but he made sure that he was buried in Canaan as he had wished.

Joseph still had his brothers and the rest of his family. 'God has saved us all by bringing us here and now I will make sure that no harm comes to you in Egypt,' he told them.

Joseph himself lived long enough to see his great, great grandchildren born. God had blessed him and all the children of Israel while they lived in Egypt. Before he died, Joseph told his brothers that God would take them back to the land of Canaan, the promised land, one day.

Thank you for my family, Lord. Help me to show each one of them that I love them.

112

Lord, open our eyes to see your love for us and respond with warm hearts.

The God who loves to give

Is there something we need to ask God to help with today?

 Isaiah 1:1–8

During the reign of King Uzziah, God spoke to a man named Isaiah and told him to talk to the Israelites.

'The special people I chose and loved and took care of no longer love me,' said God. 'Even animals show that they love their owners, but no matter what I do for my people, they turn their backs on me.

'Now they carry their sins around with them and cut themselves off from my help. Ask them if they will rebel for ever? Everything is going wrong in their lives but still they will not ask for my help.'

When love goes cold

Do we love to worship God or has it become a meaningless habit?

📖 *Isaiah 1:11-18*

'Stop bringing me sacrifices!' says God. 'I don't want to look at them. These are empty gestures – they mean nothing if you are not sorry for your sins. I hate all these things you bring to me as if you think it will make me happy. I can't hear your prayers because you say one thing and do another.

'Stop doing wicked things. Learn to do good, to be fair in all you do; help the poor, and those who are alone with no family to care for them.

'Come and talk to me,' says the Lord. 'No matter what you have done, no matter how terrible, I can take the blood red stain of your sins and make them as white as snow. Let me help you!'

Lord, forgive our sins – make them as white as snow. Lord, let our lives be full of the good things we can do for others.

Come to God!

Life on earth is short but life with God lasts for ever.

📖 *Isaiah 40:1-2, 6-11*

The prophet Isaiah spoke to the Israelites again.

'Come to me and be comforted,' says God. 'Don't be sad any more. Your sins are forgiven, you will not be punished.

'People live for a short time. Like grass they die away; like flowers they are beautiful for only a little while. Grass withers, flowers fade with time and it is the same for our short lives. But God and his words last for ever.

'God will come with power and rule with strength, rewarding people according to what they have done. He will feed his people as a shepherd feeds his flock; he will carry the lambs in his arms and gently lead the ewes with their young.'

Carry us in your arms, Lord. Lead us and keep us safe for ever.

The God of all the earth

How often do we think about just how great God is?

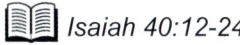 *Isaiah 40:12-24*

'God is great!' said Isaiah. 'No one else has measured the heavens or knows the weight of all the earth, the mountains and the hills. No one else can be his teacher or give him advice.

'The peoples of the world are nothing compared with God. They are but a drop in the bucket, dust on the scales.

'We cannot understand God – we cannot take in how great he is or how small we must seem compared with him. Even the great men and women we admire are as nothing compared with him. Nothing we do has any lasting worth; it all disappears. But God is God.'

Help us to remember how small we are, Lord, and how great you are.

When things can't get any worse, thank you that you are there for me, Lord.

Belonging to God

What a wonderful thought – that we are precious to God.

 Isaiah 43:1-5, 25

'Don't be afraid,' says God, 'for I have bought you with a price; I have called you by name; you are mine. 'When you go through deep waters and great trouble, I will be with you. Whatever difficulties you have, you will not be alone. When others make your life hard, you will not be destroyed by it. For I am the Lord your God: you are precious to me and I love you. Don't be afraid, for I am with you. I will take away your sins and will forget they ever happened.'

Taste and see that God is good

God promises that life with him is better than any alternative.

📖 *Isaiah 55:1-7*

God says, 'Are you thirsty? Come and drink. Even if you have no money, come and choose wine or milk. Listen well and I will tell you where you can find food that is good for your soul.

'Come to me with open ears. Listen, because what you will hear is more important than anything else you can know. What I will tell you will give you life for ever.

'I will make a promise to you; I will enter a lasting agreement to show you unlimited kindness and love. Seek the Lord while you can find him. Call upon him now while he is near.

'Stop doing things you should be ashamed of; don't even think about doing those things! Come to me so that I can be kind to you; come, so that I can forgive you.'

Lord, just as I am, I come.

Be honest in all you do…

Do we pretend, even to ourselves, that we are following God's ways?

 Isaiah 58:1-11

'Do you think you are holy because you go to Church often?' said Isaiah. '"We have fasted and prayed," you say. "We have worshipped you today." But while you are doing this you are also doing bad things in secret; you are being dishonest and unfair, you fight and quarrel.

'There is no point fasting at all when your lives carry on as if you don't know God at all. Be honest with yourselves and with God. Be generous and fair to others. Share your food with hungry people. Welcome into your homes those who have nothing. Give clothes to those who are suffering from the cold, and don't hide from your family when they need your help.

'Do these things and God will answer your prayers; God will guide you, take care of you and give you good things.'

Help us, Lord, to be honest and fair, and generous and kind, so that we worship you not only with our lips but in our lives.

Do we trust God for the future?

God has promised good things for those who love him.

📖 *Isaiah 65:17-25*

God says, 'Look! I am creating new heavens and a new earth so wonderful that no one will even think about the old ones anymore. There will be joy and happiness and the sound of weeping shall not be heard there.

'Babies will not die in their cradles and people who are 100 years old will be considered young! There will be no armies to destroy your homes and your children will not die in battle. You will live to eat the food you have grown and no one will steal it from you.

'I will answer prayers before my people even tell me their needs. The wolf and lamb shall eat together, the lion shall eat with the ox and poisonous snakes will hurt no one any more.'

Thank you for the promise of hope, of a new and better life with you in the future, with no suffering or pain.

When bad things happen...

How do we feel when God's blessings seem to stop?

📖 Exodus 1:1-22

120

Lord, help us to trust you even when things go very wrong in our lives.

Joseph's family grew and grew while they lived in Egypt, filling the land of Goshen where they lived.

Kings came and kings went until one day a new king saw that the Israelites had grown to be too many people – and he was afraid.

The king made Joseph's descendants his slaves and put hard taskmasters over them so they worked all day in the hot sun – and were exhausted. If they complained, they were beaten; if they stopped for rest, they were beaten again.

But still the Israelites grew stronger.

The king ordered the midwives to kill every baby boy who was born to the slaves to reduce their numbers. But the midwives could not do it.

So the king told his soldiers to throw every newborn baby boy born to the Israelites into the River Nile...

How does God guide us?

We must work with God to bring about the answers to our prayers.

📖 *Exodus 2:1-6, 10*

While all this was happening, Miriam's parents had a baby son. At first her mother hid the baby at home so the soldiers would not find him but as he got bigger, she needed another plan. She made a little basket from papyrus reeds and waterproofed it. She put her baby son in the basket and laid it among the reeds by the edge of the River Nile.

Miriam hid in the reeds and watched until one of the king's daughters came to the river to have a bath. When the princess heard the baby crying, she asked her maid to fetch it.

'Poor little baby,' she said. 'I will keep him for myself. His name shall be Moses.'

Help us to use the brains you have given us to make wise choices in difficult situations.

Everyone is different

The King was cruel but his daughter was kind…

 Exodus 2:7-10

Miriam came out from her hiding place and spoke to the princess.

'Do you need help to look after the baby?' she asked. 'Shall I find an Israelite mother to feed him for you?'

The princess agreed, and Miriam ran home to get her own mother!

'Take this child home and nurse him for me,' said the princess. 'I will pay you until he is old enough to come and live with me in the palace.'

So Moses was kept safe and his mother was allowed to take care of her baby son, despite the orders of the king of Egypt.

Keep us from making quick judgements about others, Lord, especially if they come from a different family or race or country.

Do two wrongs make a right?

Was Moses right to kill the Egyptian?

📖 Exodus 2:11-15

Moses grew up in the king's palace and was educated as if he were an Egyptian prince. But he never forgot he was an Israelite.

Moses could not help seeing what was happening to his people and it made him angry to see how badly they were being treated.

One day, Moses saw an Israelite slave being beaten cruelly. He looked around to see if anyone was watching – and then he killed the Egyptian slave driver and buried his body in the sand.

But someone had seen him; and soon the king found out too. Moses was so afraid that he ran away.

Help us, Lord, not to let our anger control us so that we act in the wrong way.

When there's a turn in the road

Sometimes things happen which open up new paths for us to take.

 Exodus 2:15-21

Moses kept running until he found himself in the desert of Midian where he sat beside a well.

After a while, seven young women, all sisters, came to fetch water for their father's sheep. Some shepherds chased the girls away until Moses rescued them and watered the sheep for them.

Their father, Jethro, was very grateful to Moses for helping his daughters and invited him for supper. Soon they became friends.

Moses came to live with them and married one of the young women. He started a new life as a husband and a shepherd, working for his father-in-law for many years.

Lord, help us not to dwell on the past but to take new opportunities when they arise.

When God speaks…

Do we find excuses not to do what God calls us to do?

 Exodus 2:23 – 3:13

The king of Egypt died but the Israelites were still slaves. They cried out to God to help them.

One day, while Moses was watching his sheep, he thought he saw a bush in the desert that seemed to be on fire. When he went closer, he saw that the leaves were not burning up.

Then Moses heard God's voice speaking to him from the flames.

'Moses! My people need you. They call out to me from their slavery. I want you to go to see the king of Egypt. Tell him that he must set my people free.'

'But I can't,' said Moses. 'I'm not the right person to do that! How will I know what to say?'

125

Help us to hear your voice and do as you ask. Give us willing hearts to do the job you have prepared for us, Lord.

Lord, we are weak. Take us and all we have and make us useful.

God needs us!

We may feel we have nothing to offer God but, with his help, we can do great things.

Exodus 4:10-19, 27-28

God promised to help Moses. He told him his plan to set his people free. But still Moses was afraid.

'But God,' Moses said, 'why would the king listen to me? I have never been a good speaker. Please – send someone else!'

God saw that Moses needed help. 'I will tell you what to say and the king will listen to you. But take your brother with you. I will speak to you, Moses, and Aaron will help you to speak to the king. And you will see great miracles happen.'

So Moses went to find his brother with Jethro's blessing. He met Aaron in the desert and told him everything that had happened and what God had planned for them to do.

When obedience causes pain

Doing God's will is rarely the easy route to take.

📖 *Exodus 5:1-18*

Many years had passed since Moses had been in Egypt. The old king had died.

Moses and Aaron went to see the new king, the great king of Egypt, and said, 'We have brought you a message from the God of Israel. "Let my people go," says God, "so they can worship me".'

The king was not convinced. 'Is that right?' he said. 'And who is this God that he should tell me what to do? I don't know your God and I will not let his people go. You are wasting my time!'

The king was so angry that he made the slaves work even harder than ever.

'Let them produce as many bricks as before – but now they must gather their own straw to make them!'

Guide us to do what is right and to be patient as we wait for good to come.

God is patient

How often do we demand instant answers from God?

📖 *Exodus 6:1-5, 7:14-24*

Lord, help us to understand the longer plan and to wait for answers to difficult problems.

Moses was very unhappy with what had happened. He felt he couldn't go back to the king.

'Trust me,' said God. 'The king has a hard heart but he will let my people go. They will not be slaves for ever.'

So Moses and Aaron went once more to the king and asked him to let God's people go. When he refused again, they did as God commanded them. Aaron used his special stick and the waters of the River Nile and all the canals and reservoirs turned blood red. All the fish died and no one could drink the water.

But still the king of Egypt would not let God's people go.

How well do we know God?

Moses began to learn how great God was.

📖 Exodus 8:1-10

Again Moses and Aaron went to the king of Egypt.

'Let God's people go!' they asked.

When the king refused, God sent a plague of frogs. All over the land of Egypt, loud croaking noises could be heard as frogs invaded their houses. There were frogs in the beds, frogs in the ovens and cooking bowls – there were frogs everywhere!

Then Moses and Aaron went again to the king of Egypt. 'God says, "Let my people go!"'

This time the king listened.

'Ask God to take away these frogs,' he said, 'and I will let the people go.'

'When would you like God to act?' asked Moses. 'Tell me and I will ask, then you will know that there is no one like our God.'

'Let it be tomorrow,' said the king.

Teach me to know when to speak and when to be silent, but to trust you to act.

Do we love God because he is good or because we are afraid?

Unlike the king of Egypt, who only obeyed God when it suited him, we obey him because of his love for us and ours for him.

📖 *Exodus 8:12 – 10:29*

God answered Moses' prayer and all the frogs died the following day. There were heaps of dead frogs all over the land. But as soon as the frogs had gone, the king of Egypt changed his mind. He would not let his slaves leave to worship God.

So God sent lice and flies; a plague on the animals and boils all over the people; a hailstorm that destroyed the country and locusts that stripped the land of all green leaves; then three days of deep darkness.

After each plague, the king weakened and agreed to let the people go – but as soon as God took away the plague, the king changed his mind.

Lord, help us to follow you because we love you, not only to get something we want.

How many chances do we need to trust God?

Do we need signs or miracles or can we respond to God's love?

📖 *Exodus 11:1-10, 12:1-41*

The final plague was a terrible one. There could be no more chances for the king.

God told Moses that at midnight all the first-born males in Egypt would die.

'Tell my people to prepare for a long journey,' God said to Moses, 'gathering their animals and all that they own. They must eat a meal of roast lamb, bitter herbs and bread made without yeast, and mark their doorposts with the blood of the lamb. When I see this sign, the angel of death will pass over you.'

The last plague caused much sorrow for the people of Egypt. When the king held his own son in his arms, he called for Moses and Aaron.

'Take your people and go!' he said. The Egyptians gave them silver and gold, keen to see them finally follow Moses out of Egypt.

Let us respond to your love, Lord. Draw us gently to yourself.

How do we feel when things around us change?

Can you trust God for the next step of the way or do you feel anxious about the unknown?

📖 *Exodus 13:17-22*

God had set his people free. They were no longer slaves! But this was just the beginning. As they followed Moses out of Egypt, they wondered where they would go next.

'Trust God,' Moses told them. 'We are his people. He will lead the way.'

And God did. God made a pillar of cloud for all the Israelites to follow during the day. Even the families who were travelling at the back of the long trail of people could see the cloud from far away. At night, God led them with a pillar of bright fire that shone in the darkness.

They followed, trusting God to take them to a place where they could be safe and free to worship him again.

Lord, help us to trust you for each step of the way today, even when we don't know what will happen next.

When we are afraid…

Do we call on God to help us?

 Exodus 14:5-28

The night had passed; days had followed; and the king of Egypt realized that he had let his slaves go. He was very angry. He made ready his army and all the chariots in Egypt and chased after the Israelites. They saw them in the distance while they were camped beside the sea.

The Israelites were trapped: the Red Sea was in front of them and the Egyptian army behind them. They were terrified.

'Don't be afraid,' Moses told them. 'Trust God.'

Then he held out his stick over the sea – and it parted so the Israelites could walk safely across.

When the king's chariots tried to follow, Moses raised his stick again and a flood of water washed over the Egyptians while the Israelites were safe on the other side.

Lord, bring us safely to the other side of the events that make us afraid.

Are we people who grumble?

How quickly do we turn from knowing God has blessed us to moaning about what we want next?

📖 *Exodus 15:22-27*

God was great! A miracle had occurred and God had saved his people. The Israelites were happy to be free...

But it was not long before they were hot and dusty and tired as Moses led them through the desert. They became thirsty and grumpy.

Moses told them to trust God, who had brought them across the Red Sea. Surely that same God would not let them die of thirst.

'God will give us everything we need,' said Moses.

And God did. God led them to an oasis with twelve fresh springs of water and palm trees with sweet dates to eat.

Thank you, Lord, for your many blessings. Help us to accept the bad with the good.

Do we trust God to provide for us daily?

The Israelites quickly forgot that God had answered their prayers and freed them from slavery.

 Exodus 16:1-21

The Israelites were happy that God had blessed them – for a while. They continued to follow Moses through the desert.

Then they began to grumble again.

'We were better off when we were slaves in Egypt!' they complained. 'At least we had good food to eat. I can taste the melons and cucumbers now… But here we will die from starvation!'

'Trust God,' said Moses. 'God will give us everything we need.' And God did.

Vast numbers of quails flew low over the camp in the evening so they were blessed with delicious meat; and in the morning, sweet honey-flavoured bread rained down from heaven.

Everyone had just enough to eat for that day and learned to trust God that he would provide for them the next.

Teach us to be grateful for all that you give us, Lord, day by day.

How can we live the way God wants us to?

God gave his people rules to help them live together in peace.

📖 Exodus 19:1-25

Day after day, month after month, the Israelites walked in the desert until they reached Mount Sinai. Then they camped at the foot of the mountain for three days.

Moses left the people at a safe distance at the bottom while he went up the mountain to meet with God. The mountain looked red in the sunlight but its peak had disappeared into a thick cloud of smoke.

The people heard thunder and lightning and a very loud trumpet sound – and they trembled.

And God gave to Moses rules to help them that became known afterwards as the Ten Commandments.

Thank you, Lord, that you help us by giving us guidelines to live our lives for you.

How can we show God how much we love him?

It marks us out as Christians if we show in our lives how much we love other people.

 *Exodus 20:2-17*

These are the Ten Commandments.
1. God is the only God. Love him alone.
2. Don't make idols or worship 'things' in his place.
3. Respect God's name. It is holy and special.
4. Keep the Sabbath day as a special day for rest and worship.
5. Love and respect your parents.
6. Do not murder anyone.
7. Don't steal someone else's wife or husband.
8. Do not steal anything from anyone.
9. Do not tell lies.
10. Don't be jealous of things other people have.

Lord, help me to love you as you deserve to be loved and to keep your laws.

God knows what we are like

God knows our weaknesses and faults – but we are still his people and he wants the best for us.

📖 *Exodus 21 – 24*

Help us, Lord, to act kindly and fairly to others, to be peacemakers not those who create trouble.

God explained the new laws to Moses so he could explain them to the people.

God knew that the people he had made were quick to hurt others or take things that belonged to them. God knew they could be greedy or unhappy with the things they had if someone else had more. He knew that they were afraid of people who were different from themselves and might be unkind instead of welcoming.

God's laws showed that the way to live together happily and in peace was to act kindly and justly and take care of those who could not help themselves.

How quickly do we forget our good intentions?

We need faith to wait and do things God's way.

📖 *Exodus 32:1-6*

Moses was on the mountain talking with God for a long time. The people waited below anxiously. What was happening? Would he ever come back to them?

They went to Aaron and told them their worries. They wanted to worship God but needed a god they could see.

Aaron remembered that the Egyptians had a god made in the shape of a calf. So he told them to bring all their rings and jewellery and he made them into a golden calf.

The people were very happy – now they could see the God they worshipped. They had a great feast and a party – and broke lots of God's rules while they were doing so.

Lord, we cannot see you, but we know you are real and we love you.

Are you on God's side?

Do our lives show that we belong to God?

 Exodus 32:7-35

God saw the golden calf. He saw what the people were doing and he was angry.

Moses could hardly believe what was happening. 'Forgive them,' Moses prayed to God. 'They are weak. They need to learn to trust you. Remember that you loved and cared for Abraham, Isaac and Jacob.'

Moses went down to speak to his brother and he was angry with Aaron too. 'You promised to love God – what are you doing? You have helped the people to break many of God's laws here today!'

Then Moses spoke to the Israelites. 'Who is on the Lord's side? If you want to love God and follow his ways, come with me!'

I am on your side, Lord! Let my life show it in all I say and do.

141

God offers us choices

We are not forced to follow God – it is for each of us to accept the offer he makes to us to be his friend.

Thank you for the leaders who help us to follow your ways. Lord, I want to know you better.

📖 Exodus 34:1-2, 28 ; Leviticus 1-4

God listened to Moses and he gave the people another chance to choose to love him and follow his ways. The people who were willing to follow God's laws became God's special people.

Then God gave them priests chosen from the descendants of Jacob's son, Levi. The priests were there to help them to follow the Ten Commandments and to show them how to worship God.

The priests also helped them to ask for God's forgiveness when they made mistakes or did bad things.

Keeping our side of the agreement

God is faithful to us always, all the time. Are we faithful to God?

 Exodus 25:10-22

God made an agreement with Moses and the people. It was called a covenant. God promised to take care of the people and they promised to keep his laws.

God told Moses to put the special stones on which the Ten Commandments were written into a wooden box trimmed with gold. It would be called the ark of the covenant. It had two gold rings on each side, so that it could be carried on poles wherever the Israelites went.

Help us to be faithful, Lord, remembering that we have promised to love you and do what is right and good.

The leap of faith

Sometimes we don't receive the good things God wants for us because we don't trust him to move forward.

📖 Deuteronomy 31

The Israelites walked through the desert for many years before they reached Canaan, the land God had promised them.

When they saw the land before them, Moses sent twelve spies into Canaan to find out what kind of place it would be.

Two of the men, Joshua and Caleb, told everyone that God had given them a wonderful place to live. The land was full of sweet water and good things to eat. But the other ten said that the people in Canaan were fierce and frightening – and they were afraid!

So the Israelites stayed in the desert as Moses grew older, still in sight of the land God had promised them.

Help me, Lord, to trust you, even when I am afraid.

Do we want to fit in with the crowd?

Do we live to impress others or are we happy to do the job God has given us?

📖 Matthew 3:1-4

Lord, help us to live lives that please you and not mind if that makes us different from others.

While Jesus was growing up from a boy into a man, Elizabeth and Zechariah's son, John, had grown up too. Now he was God's prophet.

John was not afraid of what people thought of him. He lived in the desert and wore an itchy shirt of camel's hair. He ate locusts and wild honey.

John was there to prepare the people to welcome the man who would show them how to be God's friends; the one who had come to save them.

He started to talk to people on both sides of the River Jordan and he baptized them as a sign that God had forgiven their sins.

Is it enough to say sorry?

John the Baptist told people to repent, to turn away from wrongdoing and do what is right.

📖 *Luke 3:3-14*

'Come and tell God you are sorry for your sins,' said John. 'Stop doing bad things. Change your ways and learn to be kind. Don't just say you love God – show it by the good things you do.

'Don't be greedy: if you have enough food, share it with anyone who is hungry; if you have more clothes than you need, give some away to people who don't have enough.

'Be honest in what you say and fair in everything you do. Don't tell lies about people. Work hard and be content with what you have.'

Men and women, soldiers and tax collectors – all sorts of people came to be baptized by John.

'I baptize you with water, but look out for someone coming soon who will baptize you with the Holy Spirit.'

Lord, make us honest and fair, kind and generous, thoughtful in all that we do.

Jesus was no ordinary man

Although he was without sin, Jesus became one of us, the people he came to save.

📖 *Matthew 3:13-17*

One day, Jesus came to the banks of the River Jordan and asked John to baptize him too.

John knew who he was immediately.

'But you have done nothing wrong!' John said. 'You don't need to say sorry. Instead, you should baptize me!'

But John did as Jesus asked. As he came up out of the water, everyone there saw the Holy Spirit come to Jesus like a dove and heard God's voice say, 'This is my Son. I love him and am pleased with what he has done today.'

Lord, may we, this day, make you pleased with all we do and say.

Do we give in too easily?

What makes it hard for us to resist temptation?

 *Matthew 4:1-11*

Jesus went into the desert and ate nothing for forty days and nights. When he was at his weakest, the devil came to persuade him to use God's power to help himself.

'If you really are God's Son, turn these stones into bread, then you won't be hungry any more,' the devil tempted him.

But Jesus did not give in to temptation.

The devil took Jesus to the very top of the temple in Jerusalem. 'If you really are God's Son, why don't you throw yourself down so God's angels will save you?'

But Jesus did not give in to temptation.

The devil took him to the top of a very high mountain. 'I will give you all that you can see, if you will bow down and worship me.'

But Jesus loved God and did not give in to temptation. Then the devil left him.

Lord, help us to know where our weaknesses lie and avoid situations where we may give in.

Is Jesus interested in all the events in our lives?

Jesus shares in our joys as well as in our sorrows.

📖 John 2:1-10

A wedding was being celebrated with a wonderful feast in the village of Cana in Galilee. Mary, Jesus' mother, and Jesus and his friends were invited along with almost everyone in the village.

After a while, Mary noticed that there was no more wine left. She was afraid the bride and groom would be embarrassed. Perhaps Jesus could help?

Jesus did not want to make a fuss but he wanted to help. He saw that there were six huge water pots standing nearby. He asked the servants to fill them to the top with water.

'Offer some to the man in charge of the feast,' Jesus said.

When the man tasted it, he saw that it was the most delicious wine! A miracle had happened! But only Mary, the servants and Jesus' friends knew how.

Be with us, Lord, to make our lives richer and better because we know you.

Life in all its fullness

Is there anything better than to know we are loved and valued by God?

📖 *John 10:7-10*

The people who listened to Jesus knew all about sheep and how they were looked after. The shepherd himself would lie across the gate to keep his sheep safe. Jesus told them that he himself was the gate and they were like the sheep.

'Those who came before me did not care about the sheep,' said Jesus. 'But those who come into the sheepfold by me will be safe. They will always find good pasture – there will be plenty to eat to keep them satisfied.

'Thieves try to steal the sheep away and kill and destroy them but I have come so that you might have life – life in all its fullness.'

Lord, we come to you, because knowing you is the best gift there can be.

Do we listen to God even when we don't like what he is saying?

The words of Jesus do not always make us feel comfortable.

📖 Luke 4:14-30

Everywhere Jesus went in Galilee, people listened to him and were amazed at what he told them. Jesus talked about God as if he really knew him. He helped them to understand how much God loved them and cared about what happened in their lives.

But Jesus had grown up in Nazareth. Here it was different.

'God has sent me to help the poor and to heal the deaf and blind,' Jesus said. 'God has sent me to show people how to live in a way that pleases him.'

But the people there shook their heads.

'What is he saying?' they said. 'Surely this is Jesus, the son of Joseph, the carpenter. We knew him when he was a boy.'

Jesus knew that he would not be accepted in the place where he had grown up.

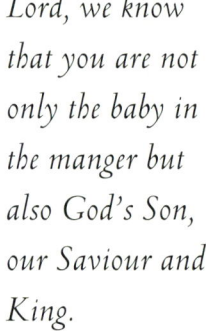

Lord, we know that you are not only the baby in the manger but also God's Son, our Saviour and King.

Will you come and follow me?

How do we respond to the call of Jesus?

📖 *Luke 5:1-11*

One day Jesus asked Simon Peter to push his boat out into deep water and do some fishing.

'Andrew and I were out all last night,' Peter told Jesus. 'There was nothing there to catch. But we'll go if you want us to...'

As soon as the brothers put the nets into the water, they were filled with so many fish that the nets began to break.

James and John saw what had happened and went to help Peter and Andrew – and soon the boats were full of silvery wriggling fish!

Now both boats were in danger of sinking with the weight of the catch of fish.

'Follow me,' Jesus said. 'Then you will catch much more than these fish.'

That day the four fishermen became the first of twelve men to become disciples of Jesus.

151

Lord, make us willing to come when you call us.

152

How can we help people to meet Jesus?

A paralyzed man's life was changed because he had friends who brought him to Jesus.

I have lots of friends who need to meet you, Lord. I want to pray for them now by name.

 Mark 2:1-4

Everyone was pleased to see Jesus in Capernaum. So when Jesus went to a house by the lake to talk to people, many came to hear what Jesus had to say. Soon the house he was in was overflowing!

There were stairs outside the house, leading to the flat roof. Soon it became clear that four men had carried their friend on a mat up the stairs and were making a hole in the roof!

When the hole was large enough, the man was lowered down. It was clear that he couldn't walk.

Why did Jesus heal people?

Jesus acted with compassion whenever he saw people who needed help.

 Mark 2:5-12

Jesus smiled at the kind friends above him. He smiled at the man who couldn't walk. Then he told the man to get up, pick up his bed, and go home. And the man did!

    The religious leaders who were there frowned and shook their heads. Did this man think he was God himself? They didn't like it at all.

    But everyone was amazed at what Jesus had done and happy that the man was healed and able to walk home.

Thank you, Lord, that you are good and kind and loving to anyone who needs your help.

154

Lord, I want to learn more about you; I want to be with other believers to know you better.

If Jesus were coming to your street today – would you want to be there?

By choosing to be where other believers are, we can learn together about God.

 *Matthew 5:1-12*

The people who heard Jesus speak, and saw the things he did, started to follow him around. They were keen to learn the things he knew about God.

Soon there was a large crowd of them. Jesus climbed the hill beside Lake Galilee and spent time talking to them.

'God will bless you if you know you need his help. God will be there to comfort you if you are sad. God will satisfy you if you long for good things and he will be kind to you if you are kind to others. God will also bless you if people are unkind to you because you love God and do good things.'

Thoughts and actions

How would you feel if people could read your mind?

 Matthew 5:13-26

'You are like the salt in the cooking pot – you make it taste better!' said Jesus. 'You are like a lighthouse, guiding ships to safety. Don't lose your saltiness! Be the people who show the world the best way to live. Don't hide your light! Let your good deeds shine out for all to see, so that people will see that God is good.

'Don't just take care about what you do, be careful about what you think. You may not actually kill someone – but being angry with them in your heart, shouting at someone or calling them names is not good either.

'Say sorry to someone you hurt before a small problem becomes a very big one.'

Forgive me, Lord, when I burn up inside because I am very angry.

I want to be perfect, Lord. Please help me…

Treating people kindly

How easy do you find it to love people if you don't think they deserve it?

 Matthew 5:38-48

Some of the things Jesus said made the people listening feel happy – Jesus told them that God cared about them. But other things were hard – God wanted things that some of them didn't find easy.

'Love other people and forgive them if they hurt you. Be generous – always give people more than they expect. Treat them the way you would like people to treat you,' said Jesus. 'Don't hate someone or pay them back if they make you sad – treat them kindly instead.

'Love your enemies and pray for them, otherwise the people who love God are no different from everyone else. Be perfect, just as God is perfect.'

Being good in secret…

Do we want to please God or feel proud because others say nice things about us?

📖 *Matthew 6:1-4*

Forgive me, Lord, when I do the right thing for the wrong reason.

'Do good things – be kind and generous,' said Jesus. 'But don't do it to be praised by other people, so they think you are an amazing person or a saint. Do it because you love God and want his love to reach out to others.

'When you help someone who is homeless or hungry, or do any other act of kindness, do it secretly so that your left hand doesn't know what your right hand is doing. Then God, who knows all secrets, will reward you.'

How should I pray?

What words should we use? What should we say?

📖 *Matthew 6:5-8*

'Talk to God in secret, as if you are talking to a father who loves you and cares about you,' said Jesus. 'Don't pray just so that other people will be impressed. Tell God that you love him. Tell him what worries you. Be honest. God will answer. He knows what you need.'

Thank you, Lord, that you are my loving father and I can tell you anything and everything.

Should I keep praying for the same thing?

Jesus once told a story to show his friends they should keep praying until they have an answer.

📖 *Luke 18:1-8*

'Once there was a man who judged between the people when they had problems. He was not a kind or generous or even friendly man. A woman who had lost her husband and was alone in the world kept coming to him, asking for his help against a man who had wronged her.

'The judge tried to ignore her. He didn't want to help her. But eventually he was so annoyed because she would not stop asking him for help that he gave in: he gave her the justice she asked for.

'If a bad, unkind man will answer someone who keeps asking for help, don't you think God, who loves you as his child, will answer you kindly when you come to him?'

I know you love me and want me to trust you. Please answer my prayers now...

Do you ever worry?

Jesus knows us and knows all the things that worry us.

 Matthew 6:25-34

'Don't worry about your life,' said Jesus. 'Don't worry so much about what you are going to eat or what you might wear… Your life is worth so much more than these things and worrying won't help you live longer.

'Look at how God feeds the birds. Look at how beautiful the flowers in the fields are. You are worth much more to God than birds or flowers and God will take care of you.

'Trust God and put him first in your life and God will make sure you have everything else you need.'

Lord, I worry about so many things. I am thinking of some of them even as I pray… Please help me to trust you more and concentrate on what really matters.

Do you believe God cares for you?

It seems amazing that the God who is creator of the world should also care for us. But he does.

📖 Psalm 8:1, 3-9

Lord, you are great and mighty, not only on the earth you have made or in the heavens above but even beyond that in places we cannot imagine!

When I think of all you have made and of all you have done, the vastness of the universe and the amazing star-studded skies, I feel very small, and can't believe that you are interested in us, in me.

Yet you created us to be like you and put us in charge of your wonderful world. Lord, you are great and mighty and the glory of your name fills the earth!

Thank you for your love, Lord. Thank you for caring about me, even me.

God's way or the world's way?

It is usually easier to follow the crowd than to do what is right.

 Luke 6:46-48

Many people listened to what Jesus said. But Jesus said it wasn't enough just to listen and nod. The important thing was to let his words change the way you acted.

'The person who acts on my words and does what is right is like a wise man who builds his house on a rock,' said Jesus. 'It may be hard work and it may take much longer, but when the storm comes and the wind howls, the wise man can sit back and know his house is safe and strong.

'Put what I say into practice and you will not be sorry. You will build your life on firm foundations.'

Help me to be wise, Lord, and go your way, even when it seems harder.

Listen to God

It feels good to live for the moment – but later we can regret not making wiser choices.

📖 *Luke 6:49*

Jesus said, 'If you listen to the things I have taught you but then choose to ignore them because the other way seems easier, you will regret it.

'You will be like a person who builds a house on the sand. It will seem easy because there is less digging to do. But as soon as the storm comes and the wind howls, the walls will fall down and the roof will fall in. Everything you have worked for will be washed away.

'Don't be foolish, be wise. Listen to me and do what is right.'

I am sorry, Lord, when I want to take the easy way instead of the best way.

God gives us strength and encouragement

God does not ask us to do things without being there to help us.

 Joshua 1:1-9

Before Moses died, God chose a new leader, one of the men who had trusted God when the spies were first sent into Canaan.

'Now that Moses is dead, you are the new leader of Israel,' God told Joshua. 'Lead my people across the River Jordan into the land I have promised will be yours. Don't worry about anything. I will always be there to help you, just as I helped Moses.

'Remember to keep my laws and remind the people to keep them too. Be strong and brave and remember that I will be with you wherever you go.'

Thank you for making us bold to do things that are right, Lord, and for always being there when we need you.

Do you judge people by where they come from?

Sometimes God chooses unexpected people to help us.

📖 *Joshua 2:1-7*

There was a big city in Canaan called Jericho. It had strong, high walls that kept the people inside safe – and kept everyone else out. Anyone who wanted to live in Canaan had first to pass by Jericho.

Joshua sent two spies into the city to find out about the people there. But the king found out there were strangers in Jericho and sent his soldiers to look for them.

'Quick! Hide here!' said a woman called Rahab. She hid the men under some flax which was drying on her roof while she sent the king's men another way. Rahab kept the spies safe until they could climb down the city wall and escape.

Lord, thank you that you choose ordinary people like me to do things to help others.

The power of God

Are we surprised when we find that people outside our faith trust God to do great things?

📖 *Joshua 2:8-15*

The spies in Jericho were very grateful for Rahab's help. The soldiers had come close to finding them. But why had she helped her enemies?

'Everyone knows about the amazing things your God has done,' Rahab told them. 'We know God led you safely out of Egypt and we know God will give you this land. Your God is God in heaven above and here on earth. I ask only this: be kind to my family. Save us as I have saved you.'

The spies promised that her family would be kept safe, and gave her a red ribbon to mark her window so they would know where they were when the time came. Then Rahab let them down the city wall by a rope.

Lord, thank you that your power can be seen throughout the world by anyone, anywhere.

Using our common sense

God expects us to take care of ourselves as well as trusting him to care for us.

📖 *Joshua 2:16-24*

Rahab left the scarlet rope hanging from the window as she had promised the spies.

Meanwhile the spies escaped from Jericho and hid in the mountains for three days so that they would not be caught. The soldiers searched for them everywhere along the road but returned without finding them.

Then the two spies came down from the mountains and crossed the River Jordan. They found Joshua and told him all that had happened.

'The people are terrified of us,' they reported. 'God has gone before us – we cannot fail to take the city and enter the land God has promised to us.'

Help me to work with you in being sensible, to look after myself and take care of those around me.

Counting our blessings

It is good to stop from time to time to recall all the times God has helped us.

 Joshua 3:1 – 4:18

Joshua had to get many thousands of Israelite men, women and children across the River Jordan to reach Jericho. God told them what to do.

The priests carrying the Ten Commandments walked into the river first. As soon as their feet touched the ground, God stopped the river flowing. The priests stood still on the river bed while all the people crossed over on dry land.

Then Joshua chose a man from each tribe to carry a stone from the middle of the river to remind them of how God had helped them safely across the River Jordan.

When the priests finally crossed over, the waters of the River Jordan flowed back.

Lord, you have done so much for me and given me so many good things. Thank you for…

Do you ever feel that what you need to do is too hard?

When we take time and space to seek God's help, he will be there to help us.

📖 *Joshua 5:13-15*

169

Thank you, Lord, that nothing is too difficult for you. Please help me today.

Joshua went out alone to plan what they should do next. He saw the high walls of Jericho in front of him – it was a strong fortress and a difficult task.

But he also saw a man with a sword in his hand.

'Who are you?' Joshua asked. 'Whose side are you on?'

'I am the captain of God's army,' the man replied.

Then Joshua knew that God would be there to help him as he had promised. He fell to his knees as he realized that this man was an angel, God's messenger, who had come with God's plan to take the city.

Are you good at keeping promises?

God wants us to be people who can be trusted to do what we promise.

📖 *Joshua 6:1-23*

The Israelites marched around the city every day for six days while seven priests marched in the middle of the army, blowing trumpets made out of rams' horns.

On the seventh day, they marched around the city six times. But on the seventh, Joshua signalled for everyone to shout with all their might!

And the walls of Jericho came tumbling down! The people of Jericho ran for their lives.

The spies who had been helped by Rahab went in to find her and brought her whole family to safety. The spies kept their promise to protect them. Her faith in God had been rewarded.

Help me, Lord, to be a person who keeps my word and does not let people down.

Sharing your faith.

Joshua's love for God led naturally to him sharing it with his people.

📖 *Joshua 23:14-16*

God gave to Joshua and the Israelites the land of Canaan, the land full of good things to eat, where they could live safely.

They spread out across the land to make their homes and farm the land; and they were happy.

Joshua knew and loved and trusted God and God blessed him so he was able to lead his people well. Before he died, Joshua encouraged them.

'God has kept all his promises to us. He loves his people. Keep his commandments always and he will bless you and take care of you.'

Lord, let me know and love you better so that others will come to know you through me.

Do you find it easy to listen to God?

God continues to love us, even if we forget him.

 Judges 4:4-10

The Israelites followed Joshua's advice for a while and listened to God. But as time passed, they forgot all the good things God had done for their ancestors. They forgot that God loved them and did not turn to him when they needed help.

Deborah was a wise woman. She still listened to God and God spoke through her so people called her a judge. The Israelites would come to her and she would guide them to do the right thing.

One day she told Barak that God wanted him to help his people by fighting the cruel Canaanite general, Sisera. Barak was frightened. He didn't trust God to help him.

'I won't go unless you come with me,' he told Deborah.

Open my ears, Lord, and let me listen. Don't let me forget how good you are to me.

How willing are we to do what God asks?

Do we make excuses and try to find a way out?

📖 *Judges 4:9-24*

Deborah trusted God.

'I will come with you,' she told Barak, 'and God will help you; but because you will not trust God, it will not be you who wins this victory. It will be a woman who takes Sisera's life.'

Deborah and Barak went into battle against Sisera and his 900 chariots. God made sure that the Israelites won the day. When Sisera saw that his soldiers were losing the battle, he escaped from the battle field and hid in Jael's tent because he thought she was on his side. But when Sisera fell asleep, Jael killed him using a tent peg.

When Barak came looking for Sisera, Jael showed him Sisera's dead body. Deborah had been right.

Lord, let me be willing to do all you ask of me.

Does God have a job for you?

We don't have to be strong, brave or very clever to do great things for God. We just have to be willing to ask for his help.

📖 Judges 6:1-16

The Israelites learned to trust God again and for a while there was peace in the land.

When they forgot about God and started to break his rules again, the Midianites attacked them, riding on camels and stealing their animals and crops.

For some years the Israelites hid from their enemies in caves until they were so hungry, they started to pray to God for help.

God answered by sending an angel to a man named Gideon, who was hiding in a winepress.

'Hello, you great soldier! God has chosen you to lead the Israelites against the enemy!' said the angel.

'Who, me?' said Gideon. 'But I am no soldier. I am no one that matters at all!'

Thank you, Lord that we all matter to you and you choose ordinary people like us to do great things.

How strong is your faith?

Some can take God at his word but others need signs and proofs to put their trust in God.

 Judges 6:36-40

The angel told Gideon that he could do anything God wanted – if he learned to trust God.

'If you really want me to lead God's army, Lord, will you help me believe? I will put a woolly fleece on the floor tonight. If there is dew on the fleece but not on the ground in the morning, I'll be sure you want me to do this.'

The next morning, Gideon squeezed a whole bowl of water out of his fleece!

'Please don't be angry with me,' Gideon said to God, 'but this time, could you make the woolly fleece dry and the ground wet?'

The next morning, the ground was wet with dew, but the fleece was perfectly dry.

Lord, you are kind and patient, even when we struggle in our faith.

The right people for the right job

God's ways are not our ways. We need to listen to what God wants us to do.

📖 *Judges 7:1-9*

Help us not to rush into things but to wait and listen so we do things your way, Lord, the best way.

Gideon was now sure that God wanted him to lead the army – and he believed that God could make miracles happen.

He gathered an army of over 30,000 men.

'Your army is too big!' God told Gideon. 'Send back anyone who is afraid.'

A lot of people went home! Then Gideon took the men who were left down to the water. Some knelt down to drink while some scooped up the water in their hands.

God told Gideon to choose for his army only the men who scooped up the water. The others were sent home. Now there were only 300 men left…

Is everything we do done to please God?

Anything we cannot say is done for God should not be done at all.

📖 *Judges 7:16-22*

Gideon divided his men into three groups. He gave each man a trumpet and a jar with a torch inside. Then, in the middle of the night, they surrounded the Midianites.

Gideon gave the signal and his men blew their horns and smashed the jars so that the light shone out. They shouted, 'A sword for the Lord and for Gideon!'

The Midianites ran in fear for their lives in every direction and began to kill each other in their confusion! So it was that God had helped the Israelites to live safely in Canaan once more.

Lord, be my guide in everything, to do even the smallest tasks the best I can.

Do we forget the good things God has done for us?

God promises that he will always be there for us, no matter how many times we forget him.

📖 *Judges 13:2-5,24; 14:6*

The next time the Israelites forgot the good things God had done, it was the Philistines who made their lives difficult.

God sent them a man called Samson, who wore his long hair in braids that had never been cut and was blessed with huge strength. Once he was attacked by a lion and killed the beast with his bare hands!

While Samson was blessed by God, the Philistines were afraid of him. They tried to think of ways to remove him so he wouldn't protect the Israelites any more.

Then they discovered Samson had a weakness – he was in love with a woman called Delilah.

Forgive us, Lord, when again and again we forget your love or take it for granted.

How well do you know yourself?

Do your weaknesses cause you to let God down again and again?

 *Judges 16*

The Philistines bribed Delilah with large sums of money to find out the secret of Samson's great strength. Delilah kept asking Samson to tell her his secret until he could stand it no longer and told her! If his hair was cut off, God would no longer bless him.

Then Delilah betrayed Samson. While Samson slept, the Philistines cut off his hair, blinded him and took him away to work in the prison. Samson's strength was gone.

One day Samson was brought out when hundreds of Philistines had come together for a feast. Samson was tied to the pillars of the building. He asked one last time for God's help, then pulled the pillars down, destroying all the people inside.

Thank you, Lord, that you know me and love me even with my faults.

Do you find it hard to be unselfish?

The apostle James encourages us to ask God for help to live good Christian lives.

 James 1:1-17

Don't give up if your life seems full of difficulties and temptations! These things will teach you patience and build your character.

If you want to know what God wants you to do, ask him, and he will gladly tell you, but trust him to answer you.

Don't worry if you feel you are not rich or powerful – God loves you just the same. Riches don't impress God and soon fade away.

Don't give in to temptations. God will never tempt you to do something wrong – but our selfishness, that desire to please ourselves, may lead us the wrong way. All good things come to us from God.

Lord, I am sorry when I am selfish and think only of myself and what I want.

Do what is right

What are the best things
we can do to show we love God?

 *James 1:19-27*

It's best to listen to others without talking too much. Try not to become angry with others: a sharp tongue is dangerous and unhelpful.

If there is something wrong in your life, give it up! You are fooling yourselves if you know what God wants you to do and then you ignore it. Instead do what is right and God will bless you.

God wants our lives to shine out with good things – don't try to be like the people around you who don't care about God. The very best things we can do are to take care of children who have no families or older people who are lonely and need looking after.

Lord, help us to give up anything that stops us doing what is right.

Help me always to follow your example in the way I treat others.

What would Jesus do?

If we are unsure of the right way to act, think of the example Jesus gave us.

 James 2:1-4, 8-13

'Do you treat rich people better than poor people?' asked James. 'If a man comes into Church dressed in expensive clothes and another comes in looking as if he is homeless, are you kinder to the rich man than the poor man? What do you think Jesus would have done?

'Isn't it better to love and help your neighbours just as much as you love and take care of yourself, as Jesus taught?

'If you are perfect in every way but are not kind to the poor, you are just as guilty as if you have murdered someone. Do what Jesus wants you to do. Take care both how you think and how you act.'

Does God care more about what we believe or what we do?

James is clear about what real faith means.

📖 *James 2:14-20*

'What good is your faith if it isn't worked out in the way you behave towards others?' said James. 'If you have a friend who is in need of food and clothing, and you say, 'God bless you,' but don't help him in some practical way, your faith is dead and useless.

  'The way to God is indeed by faith alone – you can do nothing to save yourself; Jesus has done it all for you. But if you have faith, good things always come from that – people should be able to see we have faith by the way we act. If faith is not followed by good actions, it is not real faith at all.'

May all I believe and all that I do show that I love you, Lord.

None of us knows what the future holds

How would we feel if all that we valued was taken from us?

 Ruth 1:1-12

There was a famine in the little town of Bethlehem. People were hungry. So Elimelech took his wife Naomi and his two sons to live in Moab.

After some time, Elimelech died and Naomi's sons married. Naomi still had a family to care for her. Then both her sons died too – and the three women were left alone.

Naomi was very sad. Her family meant everything to her.

She decided to return to Bethlehem where she knew the famine had ended. She told Orpah and Ruth to go home so they could find new husbands and have families of their own. Then they at least could be happy again.

Help us to be thankful for what has passed, trust you for all that is to come and live for today.

How loyal are we to those we love?

Ruth loved Naomi and was determined to stay and take care of her.

 Ruth 1:14-18

Naomi's two daughters-in-law cried with her. They didn't want to leave her. But eventually Orpah was persuaded and she left and went home to her mother.

Ruth would not go. She begged to stay with Naomi.

'Don't make me go,' Ruth said. 'My home is with you now. I will go where you go and live where you live. Your people will be my people and I will worship your God. I want to die wherever you die and then I shall be buried there too. Let only death separate us in the future.'

Naomi was very glad of Ruth's love and kindness and she agreed. So it was that Naomi and Ruth went together to Bethlehem to make a new home there.

Make our love strong, Lord, so that we take care of our family when they most need our help.

Is God guiding our steps today?

God led Ruth to a place where she was helped and protected.

 Ruth 2:1-12

Naomi had a relative in Bethlehem called Boaz. When Ruth went out to gather the leftover grain from the harvest so that they would have enough to eat, she found herself working in one of his fields.

Boaz asked one of his men about her.

'She came back from Moab with Naomi,' he was told. 'She has been working hard all day with almost no rest.'

When Boaz heard how kind Ruth had been to stay with Naomi, he spoke kindly to her.

'Gather as much grain as you need,' he said. 'My men will be kind to you. You have come here to live among strangers and now God will bless you.'

Guide our steps, Lord, and lead us where you want us to go.

God's care and protection

Ruth was a stranger but God welcomed her into his family.

 *Ruth 2:14-23*

When lunchtime came, Boaz invited Ruth to join them. He made sure she had plenty to eat and when she went back to work, he told his men to drop more grain so that she could pick it up.

When Ruth returned in the evening, Naomi was amazed at how much grain she had collected.

'And look, I have brought you some of the food Boaz gave me for lunch too. There was too much for me to eat! He told me I would be welcome to go back tomorrow.'

Naomi clapped her hands with joy. She smiled wider than she had in a long time.

'This is God's doing,' she told Ruth. 'He is taking care of us both.'

Ruth stayed and worked in Boaz's fields throughout the harvest.

Help us to welcome strangers, Lord, and to show your love to them.

Does God have plans for good?

Ruth was a stranger but she became the ancestor of kings.

📖 Ruth 3:1-2, 4:13-17

One day, Naomi sat Ruth down and smiled.

'What do you think about getting married again?' she said. 'Boaz is such a kind man and he has been good to us both. I think if we asked him, he would make you his wife and take care of you.'

Boaz had already seen that Ruth was good and kind and loyal. Naomi knew that he wanted Ruth to be his wife.

So it was arranged and Ruth became the wife of Boaz. God soon blessed them with a son and Naomi was happy when she held her little grandson in her arms.

Their son Obed later became the father of Jesse; and even later, the grandfather of David, who was to become King of Israel.

Thank you, Lord, that you can see the future and bring good things out of bad.

God's everlasting love

The apostle Paul believed in God's great plan for each of us.

 Romans 8:26-37

'If we trust God, the Holy Spirit will guide our prayers and lead us when we don't even know what to pray for. He will help us to find what God's will is.

'If we love God, all that happens to us can be woven into that plan so that good things are the result.

'God knew that he would be welcoming us into his family from the very beginning. It's an amazing fact! And if God is on our side, what does it matter if anyone else is against us?

'When things go wrong, it doesn't mean that God doesn't love us. If we are hungry or have no money, if we are in danger or even threatened with death, it doesn't mean God has deserted us.

'Nothing can ever separate us from God's love, nothing at all.'

Thank you, Lord, that wherever we are or however we feel, nothing can come between us and your love.

Are we always willing to help others?

Jesus was concerned for everyone, whoever they were and whatever others thought about them.

📖 *Matthew 8:1-4*

When Jesus came down from teaching on a hillside in Galilee, there were many people following him. Just then a leper came timidly towards Jesus. He knelt on the ground in front of him.

'I know who you are,' the man said. 'I know that if you wanted to help me, if you wanted to heal me, you could.'

The man at Jesus' feet was scarred by his terrible skin disease. But Jesus touched him.

'I want to help you,' he said. 'Be healed.'

And that moment a miracle happened: the man's skin became clean again.

'Go straight to the priest,' Jesus told him, 'so he can see you are well. Take with you an offering so he knows you were a leper who has been healed – and then you can be part of the community again.'

Help me, Lord, to want to help anyone who needs me and not look the other way.

Amazing faith

We will never know whether God can help us if we do not come to him and ask…

 Matthew 8:5-13

When Jesus went to Capernaum, he met a Roman soldier who asked for his help. He was a good man who had built a synagogue for the local people.

'Please will you help?' the soldier said. 'My servant is in great pain.'

'I will go and heal him. Show me the way,' he said.

The soldier shook his head. 'I don't deserve you to come to my house,' he said. 'But I know you can heal my servant. Just say he is healed and I know that he will be.'

Jesus had never seen such faith before, even among the Jewish people. 'God welcomes people everywhere to believe and you clearly trust God,' Jesus said. 'Go home now. Your servant is well again.'

When the man returned to his house, his servant had been healed.

Lord, I believe. Help me when I doubt you…

Do we care about people the way that God does?

Jesus saw people in all kinds of need and his heart was always deeply moved.

 Luke 7:11-17

When Jesus and his friends went to visit the village of Nain in Galilee, a crowd of people followed him.

At the gates of the town they met a funeral procession. The body of a young man was being carried away to be buried. His mother, a widow, was weeping for her only son.

Jesus saw how sad she was. He knew that now she would be quite alone.

'Don't cry,' he said to her. Jesus touched the dead man – and life flowed back into him. The woman was overjoyed! Her son was alive!

But the people around were amazed. 'God has come to help his people,' they said.

The news of what Jesus had done began to spread to people all over the land.

Lord, I want to care in the same way that you do. Give me a loving, generous heart.

The gift of God's forgiveness

How much do we love God for all he has done for us?

 *Luke 7:36-47*

Jesus was eating with one of the Pharisees when a woman came into the house. She knelt behind Jesus, weeping, with her tears falling on his feet. She wiped them off with her hair before pouring perfume over them.

The Pharisee was shocked.

'Simon,' Jesus said, 'let me tell you a story. A man once lent money to two people, £5000 to one and £500 to the other. Neither could pay him back, so the man said that neither had to pay him a penny. Who loved him most after that?'

'The one who had owed him the most?' Simon answered.

'That's right,' Jesus agreed. 'Now this woman has washed and dried my feet and anointed them with oil. I am your dinner guest – but she has taken better care of me than you have. She has done many wrong things but I forgive her everything. She loves me more than you do because of it.'

Thank you for your forgiveness, Lord. Let me love you more and more.

Putting God first

Would you do anything to belong in God's kingdom?

 Matthew 13:44

Jesus often told stories or parables to help people understand what he was saying. Sometimes the meaning was clear and other times they still needed help to understand.

'God's kingdom is like buried treasure in a field,' Jesus once said. 'When a man found this treasure, he sold everything he had to buy the field so that he could own the precious treasure.

'God's kingdom is precious in the same way. It is worth all you have. Do whatever you can to follow God's way. Nothing is more important. It's the best thing you will ever do.'

Help me to follow your way, Lord, today and every day.

Trusting God

Do we find it easy to trust God when we are afraid?

📖 *Luke 8:22-25*

One day Jesus told his disciples to cross to the other side of Lake Galilee. They all got into the fishing boat and Jesus put his head on a pillow to rest. He was so tired, he quickly fell asleep.

Suddenly a storm blew up. The little fishing boat was tossed high on the rough waves. Water began to slosh over the sides and into the boat.

'Master! Wake up!' the disciples shouted. 'Help us or we will drown!' They were terrified.

Jesus stood up and shouted over the sound of the wind. 'Peace, be still!'

Almost as suddenly as it had begun, the storm had gone. The disciples were amazed.

'Didn't you trust me to save you?' Jesus asked them.

Lord, let me put my hand in yours when everything around me is stormy.

Do we ask God to help others?

Jairus asked for help for his daughter; the woman came to Jesus so he would heal her.

📖 *Luke 8:40-48*

One day a man called Jairus came to ask Jesus for help.

'Please come to my house!' he begged. 'My only child is very ill. She is only twelve and I think she is dying!'

Jesus went quickly with Jairus, moving through the thick crowd of people.

But there was in the crowd a woman who had been ill for twelve years. She needed Jesus' help too. If only she could touch his robe…

Suddenly Jesus stopped. 'Who touched me?' he asked.

Then he smiled at the woman. He knew what had happened. 'It's OK,' said Jesus. 'Your faith has healed you.'

Lord, I need you today but I also pray for the people I know who need you, too…

The difference that Jesus makes

When everyone else has given up, Jesus is there to change things.

📖 *Luke 8:49-56*

As Jesus went to help Jairus' daughter, someone pushed through the crowd towards them.

'It's too late,' the man said to Jairus. 'I'm so sorry but your daughter has just died…'

Jesus took Jairus by the arm. 'Don't worry; just trust me,' said Jesus.

When they arrived at the house, Jesus sent away all the weeping women. Only the girl's parents and three of his disciples went into the room with him.

'Get up, little girl,' Jesus said. Jairus' daughter opened her eyes and sat up. 'I think she's hungry,' smiled Jesus. 'She needs some food.'

Jairus and his wife were overjoyed! Their little girl was well again.

Lord, be here with us now, to help and heal, to comfort and give us hope, even when things are really bad.

What is God's love like?

It's amazing – a love that sent Jesus to die for people who don't even want to know him.

📖 *John 3:1-17*

Thank you for your amazing love, Lord – and a chance to start again.

The religious leaders did not like Jesus. But Nicodemus was not like the others. He was curious. He was interested. He was amazed at what Jesus taught about God. He wanted to know more but he didn't want everyone to know that he had spoken to Jesus.

So Nicodemus came to see him secretly, at night.

'God sent me here to save people,' Jesus told him. 'God loves the world he has made so much that he has given his only son to save them. Anyone who believes in me will live for ever. But it is like being born a second time. Everything is new. You can start all over again.'

Is knowing Jesus worth telling others about?

The life Jesus offers us is so good we want to pass it on.

 *John 4:4-30*

It was very hot, and as Jesus and his disciples passed through Samaria, Jesus sat by the well while his friends went to find some food.

Most people were in the shade away from the heat but one woman came to draw water from the well.

'Would you give me some water?' Jesus asked her.

The woman was grumpy. 'I don't know why you are asking me – you Jews don't usually talk to Samaritans,' she replied.

'I know everything about you,' said Jesus. 'I can give you sweet, bubbling water that will stop you ever being thirsty again. I am the one you are waiting for, sent by God to save you.'

The woman was so amazed, she ran off to tell everyone she saw that Jesus, the Saviour, was here.

Thank you for the gift of life, worth more than anything else.

200

Have you ever done something wrong?

You are not alone! And for that reason, we should not judge other people.

📖 John 8:3-11

Lord, I know that I am not perfect. Help me to see the good in everyone and not be quick to criticize others.

Some of the religious leaders brought to Jesus a woman who had stolen someone else's husband. They wanted to trick him.

'Teacher,' they said to Jesus, 'this woman has done a terrible thing. The law given to Moses says we should stone her to death. What do you think?'

'You may stone her until she dies,' said Jesus after a moment. 'But the person who throws a stone at her first must be the one who has never sinned.'

One by one, the Jewish leaders walked away until only Jesus was left with the woman.

'Did no one condemn you?' he asked the woman.

'No, sir,' she said.

'Neither do I,' said Jesus. 'Go and don't do the same thing again.'

The importance of hope

Jesus changes things, making sense of our lives and giving us purpose.

📖 *John 8:12-18*

'I am the light of the world,' said Jesus to a crowd of people. 'If you follow me, you won't have to walk in darkness any more because I will bring light and hope into your lives. I will show you where things have gone wrong but I will also show you that God is loving and will forgive you if you come to him.'

The Pharisees didn't like this. They thought it wrong that Jesus should say this about himself.

'I know where I came from and where I am going,' Jesus said to them. 'God the Father sent me and is with me now and he knows that what I have said is true.'

201

Thank you for bringing light into the darkness, Lord, and giving me hope and purpose.

202

Do we sometimes make bargains with God?

Be honest when you pray: pour out your heart; tell God what you feel.

Lord, please hear me as I tell you now the things I can share with no one else...

 1 Samuel 1:1-20

Hannah wanted a baby very much.

Everyone she knew had a baby and some had lots of babies – but although she and her husband loved each other very much, no babies came.

Hannah prayed all the time that God would bless them with a child; then she prayed that if God blessed her with a baby son, she would let him train in the temple to serve God there all his life.

She told Eli, the priest, what she had prayed for.

'May God bless you, and give you the child you want so much,' he said.

When prayers are answered...

God gives good gifts to his children.

 *1 Samuel 1:21-28*

God heard Hannah's prayers and he answered her.

Soon she found that she was expecting her first child and before long she gave birth to a baby son. She was the happiest wife in Israel when she held baby Samuel in her arms!

Hannah loved him and looked after him well but when he was big enough, she took him to live in the temple, just as she had promised.

There Samuel learned how to love God and serve him with the help of Eli, the priest.

But God did not forget Hannah. God blessed her with another three sons and two daughters.

Thank you, thank you, thank you, Lord, for all the prayers you have answered — and for the things I am so grateful for today...

Do we expect God to speak to us?

God speaks in many ways: sometimes through the words of the Bible or through other people.

 1 Samuel 3:1-10

Eli, the priest, was very old and almost blind. He was grateful for Samuel's help in the temple.

One night, Samuel heard a voice calling him. He went to Eli. 'Here I am!' he said. 'You called me.'

But Eli had been asleep. 'I didn't call you. Go back to your bed,' he said.

A little while later, Samuel heard the voice again. Samuel went again to Eli. 'Here I am!' he said. 'You called me.'

But Eli had not called. He sent him back to bed.

When it happened a third time, Eli sat up and thought. 'God is speaking to you, Samuel,' he said. 'When he speaks to you again, tell him you are listening.

God did call Samuel again. Samuel answered, and he listened. And God began to tell Samuel his plans for the people of Israel.

Speak, Lord, in the stillness and hush our hearts to listen.

Do we believe God wants what is best for us?

It's easy to believe when we get what we want, but what happens if we don't?

 *1 Samuel 3:10-21*

As the years passed, everyone knew they could trust Samuel. When God spoke to him, he listened. Then Samuel told the people what God wanted them to do. They understood that what God wanted for them was good – he was like a father who takes good care of his children.

With God's help, Samuel organized the Israelites into an army to stop the fierce Philistines on their borders from attacking them.

For as long as Samuel was God's prophet, there was peace in the land. The people were happy.

Thank you, Lord, for caring for us like a good father to his children.

Do we want to be like everyone else?

We are set apart when we trust God, with different values and standards from others.

 1 Samuel 8:1-19

When Samuel became an old man, his sons became judges in his place. But they were greedy and the people of Israel were not happy.

'All the other nations around us have a king,' they said. 'We want you to choose a king to rule us instead.'

Samuel was unhappy about this. He asked God what to do.

'They are rejecting me, not you,' said God. 'They can have a king if that's what they want. But warn them what will happen.'

Samuel told the people that a king would take their sons away into battle or make them work in his fields; he would take their best land and some of what they grew in taxes.

'Are you sure you want to be like the other nations?' Samuel asked.

'Yes!' the people answered.

Lord, be king of our lives in all we do today.

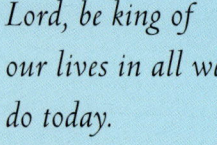

Asking for guidance

Are we too proud to ask someone wiser to help us?

📖 *1 Samuel 9:1-20*

Samuel knew that God would help him find a man who would be the first king of Israel.

One day, Saul came to him. Saul was very tall and handsome, the son of a very rich man named Kish. He had been searching for his father's donkeys which had wandered off and thought Samuel – a prophet – might be able to help.

'Can you tell me where to find Samuel?' Saul asked him.

Samuel smiled. 'I am Samuel,' he said. 'You have found me. Stop worrying about your donkeys, Saul, because they have been found. But there is a much more important job for you to do.'

Samuel knew that God had chosen Saul to be the king the people wanted.

Thank you for leaders and teachers who help us to discover God's will for us.

How would you respond if God called you to a huge task?

God often chooses those who feel they have little to offer to do great things.

📖 *1 Samuel 9:21 – 10:1*

Samuel knew that God had chosen Saul, but Saul was sure he had the wrong man!

'But why me?' Saul said. 'I am no one – I am less than no one! My family is not important and I have no special gifts. Why would God choose me?'

Saul had a meal with Samuel and he and his servant stayed the night. But in the morning Samuel sent Saul back to his father. He walked with him a little way and then sent the servant on ahead.

'You are the man God has chosen to be king,' Samuel said, and he poured holy oil on his head.

Lord, make us ready to do anything you ask of us.

The power to change

How willing are we to let God change us?

📖 *1 Samuel 10:3-11*

Samuel told Saul where he should go and what would happen next.

'You will meet a band of prophets coming down the hill playing music and speaking about what God will do as they come. Then God will give you power to be the king he wants you to be. You will feel like a different person; you will act like a different person and God will guide you to make good decisions.'

It all happened just as Samuel had said. God blessed Saul to be the first king of Israel and he knew that he was a changed person.

Spirit of the Living God, fall on us and change us to be the people you want us to be.

210

God does not give up on us

God is the same, yesterday, today and forever – even when we forget the good things he has done for us.

 1 Samuel 10:17-27

Lord, we want to remember now the good things you have done for us this week.

A week later, Samuel gathered the twelve tribes of Israel to show them their new king.

'God has listened to you,' he said. 'Once you were slaves in Egypt – but God listened when you called to him and he rescued you! Now you have rejected him. You have asked for a king to help you; you decided God was not enough.

'Now we will see the king God has chosen to lead you.' But Saul was not there! He was so nervous, he was hiding!

When they found him and Saul stood up in front of everyone, the people were delighted with the king God had chosen.

'Long live the king!' they shouted.

Do you always want things your own way?

It's easy to do as God asks us for a while; it's more difficult to keep on to the end.

 *1 Samuel 15:1-35*

Saul listened to God and led his people well. Soon Israel was respected among the nations around them; people were afraid to fight them. Everyone was happy.

'Don't forget how God has taken care of you in the past,' said Samuel. 'Remember to love him and follow the Ten Commandments. Then God will bless you.'

But after some time, King Saul forgot that he was God's king. He knew the people loved him. He stopped doing things God's way and did as he liked. Then he stopped listening to God.

Samuel was disappointed. 'What have you done?' he asked Saul. 'If you will not listen to God, he will find another man who will…'

Help us to value what you think of us rather than look for the approval of the people around us.

Do we judge people by how they look?

God teaches us to look for kindness and wisdom not just what we see on the outside.

 1 Samuel 16:1-11

Samuel knew that God wanted a king who would be wise and do what was right. So he wasn't surprised when God sent him to Bethlehem to meet a man named Jesse.

Jesse introduced the eldest of his sons. He was tall, strong and handsome.

'This must be the one God has chosen,' Samuel thought.

'Don't judge by what you see on the outside,' said God. 'I see what people are like when no one is looking at them.'

Jesse introduced his second son, also tall, strong and handsome. But he was not God's chosen king.

Samuel met Jesse's third, fourth, fifth, sixth and seventh sons. They were all tall, strong and handsome; but none of them was God's chosen king.

Lord, help us not to make judgements about anyone based only on what we can see.

The God of surprises

No one had thought to invite David to meet Samuel; but God already had plans for him.

📖 *1 Samuel 16:12-13*

Jesse was surprised that none of his sons older had been the man that Samuel was looking for. Samuel was surprised too.

'Do you have any more sons?' Samuel asked.

'My youngest son, David, is taking care of the sheep.' Jesse replied. 'I will send someone for him.'

When Samuel met David, God said, 'This is the one I have chosen. This is the next king of Israel.'

So Samuel anointed David with oil, as a sign that one day he would be king.

Thank you, Lord, that you see beyond our imagination and understanding. Surprise us today!

214

God's goodness

Are we as certain of God's love and protection as David was when he was a shepherd boy?

 Psalm 23

'Because the Lord is my shepherd, I have everything I need,' sang David.

'He lets me rest in green meadows and leads me beside quiet streams. He gives me strength when I am weary. He helps me to do what is right and good.

'Even when death draws near I don't need to be afraid, because God is close beside me, taking my hand so I am not alone and guiding me all the way.

'God blesses me with good things even in difficult times. I can trust him to be kind to me all the days of my life and afterwards I will live with him forever in his home.'

Thank you that you are my shepherd, Lord, and you take care of me too. Help me to be sure of your love and kindness every day of my life.

What will heaven be like?

John, one of Jesus' special friends, had a vision of what we might expect in heaven.

 *Revelation 21:1-4*

'In my vision I saw a new sky and a new earth without any sea. Everything I had known before had disappeared. I saw the Holy City, the new Jerusalem, coming down from God out of heaven. And it was beautiful.

'I heard a loud voice saying, "Look, God's home is right here: God will live with the people he has made and they will be his friends. He will not be distant or invisible or ever seem far away.

'"God will wipe away all tears from their eyes, and there shall be no more pain or suffering, no more sadness or crying, no more death or dying. All of that has gone forever."'

Thank you, Lord, that I don't need to be afraid of death, whenever it comes, because you will be there with me.

The difference that faith makes

Saul no longer trusted God and was moody and grumpy, while David knew that God was his friend.

 1 Samuel 16:14-18

King Saul couldn't sleep. He was grumpy and shouted at everyone. No one could do anything right.

Then one of his servants said, 'I know a young man who loves God and plays music on the harp. Perhaps that would help you to sleep?'

So David was brought to King Saul's court to play his harp.

Saul liked David. His music soothed the king. 'David can take care of my armour,' he said. 'Then he can be here whenever I need him.'

You are my friend, Lord, and knowing you makes me happy. Thank you!

Is our faith more than just words?

There's a difference between saying the right things, and believing, so that we act in the right way.

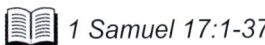 1 Samuel 17:1-37

The Philistines had a champion fighter, a huge giant of a man named Goliath. Day by day, Goliath marched up and down and shouted at the Israelites.

'Send out a man to fight me,' he boomed. 'Whoever wins will make slaves of the rest!'

David heard the giant's challenge; he saw that his brothers, who were soldiers, and even King Saul himself, trembled when they heard Goliath.

'If no one else will go, I will fight this bully!' he said.

'But you are just a young man – and he is a trained warrior,' said King Saul.

'God has kept me safe from lions and bears when I took care of my father's sheep. God will take care of me now,' said David.

Lord, may the faith we have in you make us do the right things – whatever the cost.

218 Do we trust God to help us?

Sometimes the simple faith of younger people is stronger than that of those who have known God a long time.

 1 Samuel 17:38-50

Lord, whatever age we are, let us not forget that you are the God of all the world – and you want to help us.

King Saul offered David his helmet, but it was far too big. He offered David his armour, but it was far too heavy. Even the sword was too uncomfortable for David to use.

So David took his sling and found some stones from the stream. Goliath was angry when he saw him coming out to meet him – were the Israelites mocking him by sending out a boy?

'You may have better weapons and armour,' said David, 'but I have the God of all the world to help me!'

Then David swung the sling around his head so that the stone hit Goliath in the forehead. The giant fell down with a thud. The Israelites cheered! David had defeated the giant!

Does knowing God bring us joy?

David celebrated God's presence with food and music and dancing – he was really happy.

📖 *2 Samuel 5:1-4, 6:1-5, 17-19*

David grew to be a good soldier and a great leader.

When Saul died, the people asked David to be their king. They loved him. He was not only strong and brave but he loved God. They knew that God wanted him to take care of them as a shepherd cares for his sheep.

For a while, there was peace again in the land. David brought the ark of the covenant to the city of Jerusalem and made this the place where he lived. It was a time of great joy and celebration with music and dancing.

Help us, Lord, to know deep down joy in our hearts that we know you and that you are with us.

220

Have you ever wanted something that belongs to someone else?

Even when God has given us many good things, we are often greedy for something more.

📖 2 Samuel 11:1-27

David had been king for a long time. God had blessed him with wives and children and many victories in battle.

One night, while his army was away at war, David saw a beautiful woman from his rooftop. He found out that she was Bathsheba, the wife of Uriah, one of his soldiers.

David wanted very much to meet Bathsheba. Then, when he had met her, he decided he couldn't live without her. He wanted her to be his wife.

David sent a message to one of his commanders to make sure that Uriah was in the most dangerous part of the battlefield. Then when the news came that Uriah had been killed, David married Bathsheba.

David had done a terrible thing.

Forgive me when I am greedy for what someone else has, Lord. Thank you for your many blessings.

Do you find it easy to admit to mistakes you have made?

God knows our hearts; we cannot hide from him.

 2 Samuel 12:1-7

David knew that he had stolen another man's wife. He knew he had arranged his death. He knew he had done something very wrong and he hoped no one else would find out.

But God knew what David had done.

God sent Nathan the prophet to David. Nathan told David a story about a very rich man who had everything – but he was still greedy for more. So he stole a poor man's only lamb. David was very angry.

'That's terrible!' David said. 'That rich man deserves to die!'

Nathan looked David in the eye. 'But you are that rich man,' he said.

Lord, I know I am not perfect and that no secrets can be hidden from you. Help me to come to you to say sorry.

Can you be honest when you talk to God?

Facing up to our mistakes can be very painful.

 2 Samuel 12:6-12

When Nathan had finished speaking to him, David saw himself for the first time the way that God saw him.

He had used his power as king to get what he wanted. He had broken God's rules by stealing Bathsheba from her husband and arranging his death. He had been greedy and selfish and had behaved as if he didn't know or love God at all.

David had done so many terrible things, he put his head in his hands and he cried.

Lord, I am so sorry for the wrong things I have done. Thank you that you are a kind and forgiving God.

Are you ever afraid God will turn his back on you?

When we are really sorry, God knows we mean it.

📖 *Psalm 51*

David poured out his heart to God in his sorrow.

'Lord, I am so, so sorry. Please be kind to me because I know your love is beyond my understanding. Wash away these terrible things I have done.

'I know what they are – I can think of nothing else. I don't deserve anything from you, but I know how good you are; I know that you can forgive me and it will be as if I have been washed clean again. You can make me happy where all I feel now is deep sadness. Make my heart pure again, Lord. Help me and don't leave me.

'Lord, I am broken. Please mend me.'

Thank you that you never turn us away when we come and say sorry.

224

Learning to forgive yourself

Do you see things that go wrong in your life as God's punishment?

📖 2 Samuel 12:13-24

'God is very sad because of what you have done,' Nathan told David. 'But he will not hold this against you for ever. God will forgive you.'

Not long afterwards, Bathsheba gave birth to a baby son. But the baby became very ill. Despite David's prayers, he died, and David blamed himself for this. He thought it was all his fault, that God was punishing him and he became depressed.

Time passed and God blessed David and Bathsheba with another son. David began to be happy again.

They named their son Solomon.

Thank you, Lord, that you forget our sins and do not hold them against us.

What is God like?

We cannot grasp just how much more generous God is than we are!

📖 *Psalm 103*

I will bless God's holy name with all my heart. I will never forget the blessings he showers on me.

God forgives my sins and heals me. He surrounds me with love and fills my life with good things! He is kind and gentle even when we don't deserve it; he is slow to get angry and full of love.

God never bears a grudge, or remains angry for ever. He has removed our sins as far away from us as the east is from the west. He is like a father to us, knowing our days are few and brief, like grass or wild flowers, blown by the wind then gone for ever.

Let everything everywhere bless the Lord, just as I bless him too.

Lord, you are good and kind and generous and loving. Make me more like you, day by day.

226

What does God need to forgive in your life?

King David had not always followed God's ways. Just like us, he did things that made him ashamed.

 1 Kings 1:38-40, 2:1-12

As David grew nearer to the day of his death, he wanted to give his son some good advice.

'Love God and keep his commandments and you will do well,' he said. 'There is nothing more important than that.'

David remembered how much he had loved God when he was a young man and the mistakes he had made as he grew older. He wanted Solomon to be a better king than he felt he had been.

In time Solomon was anointed with oil and declared king, just as his father had been before him.

Lord, I am sorry when I let you down. Make my heart good and kind.

How does God bless people who put him first?

Solomon knew that serving God was the most important thing he could do with his life.

📖 1 Kings 3:5-15

One night in a dream, God said to Solomon, 'Ask for anything you like and I will give it to you.'

Did Solomon ask to be rich or famous or to live a long life? No, Solomon did not think of himself.

'Please give me a wise heart, so that I can help your people,' Solomon prayed.

God was pleased with his answer. He gave Solomon the gift of wisdom so he became the wisest man ever – and made him rich and famous too!

Help me, Lord, to offer my whole life to you and to know your blessing in everything I do.

228

Do we use the gifts God gives us?

Solomon helped others by putting his gifts to good use.

📖 1 Kings 3:16-28

One day two young women came to see Solomon.
   Both women lived in the same house and had given birth to baby boys. One of the babies had died.
   'The living baby is mine,' said one of the women. 'She put her dead child in my arms while I slept.'
   'No, her son died and mine is the living child,' said the other.
   'Cut the baby in half,' Solomon said. 'Then you can share it.'
   'No! She can have the baby,' said the first woman. The other said, 'Yes, then neither of us can have him!'
   Solomon gave the baby to the first woman because she wanted him to live. 'This is the child's mother,' he said. Everyone was amazed and saw that God had blessed Solomon.

Help us to see what gifts you have given us – and then to use them for the good of all.

Where does God live?

Solomon knew God was too great to live in any building.

📖 1 Kings 5:13 – 8:61

When Solomon built the temple, it took thousands of men seven years to complete. Solomon panelled the stone walls with wood covered with gold and decorated them with carved flowers and golden angels.

When it was finished, it was beautiful. Solomon called all the people together and prayed.

'Lord, there is no one like you – loving and kind, great and mighty! There is nowhere good enough for you to live – not even this beautiful temple.

'But let your people come to worship you here. Let them ask for your help in their need, and for your forgiveness for their wrongdoings. Be with us, Lord, and never leave us. May everyone know that you alone are God – and be filled with the desire to live good and perfect lives.'

Thank you for your help and your forgiveness, Lord. Give us the desire to live good and perfect lives.

230

Sometimes I feel as if I have nothing to offer, Lord. Thank you that, with your help, even the smallest gift can be used to help others.

What gifts can we offer to Jesus?

Jesus can use anything we bring to him to make great things happen.

 John 6:1-13

Jesus had been talking to a crowd of over 5,000 people and he had healed people who had come to him for help. But now it was late. Jesus saw that people were hungry and far from their homes.

'Where can we find food for everyone here?' Jesus asked his disciples.

'This boy has brought us five pieces of bread and two fishes,' said Andrew, 'but that won't go far...'

The disciples told everyone to sit down while Jesus thanked God for the food. Jesus broke the bread and fish into pieces and gave them to the disciples to share with everyone.

When they had eaten enough, there were still twelve baskets of leftovers. It was a miracle!

Do you find it hard to trust Jesus?

Our faith may be stronger when we stop letting everyday problems get in the way.

 Matthew 14:22-31

The disciples were sailing across Lake Galilee in the moonlight. Jesus had stayed behind to pray for a while. When the boat was a long way from the shore, the men in the boat saw someone coming towards them, walking on the water.

'Don't be afraid,' Jesus shouted. 'It's me!'

Peter stood up in the boat. 'Lord, if it's really you,' he said, 'let me come to you across the lake.'

Peter stepped out on to the water and started to walk towards Jesus. But the wind blew and Peter took his eyes off Jesus. He began to sink.

Jesus caught his hand and helped him back into the boat. 'Why were you afraid, Peter?' Jesus asked. 'Didn't you trust me?'

I want to trust you, Lord, to help with all those things that seem so hard today.

How do I show that I love God?

Do we love God in all we say and do – or choose to keep God out of some parts of our lives?

📖 *Luke 10:25-29*

A man once asked Jesus how he could best show God that he loved him.

'What do the scriptures teach you?' asked Jesus.

'I know I must love God with all my heart and soul and strength – with every part of me,' said the man. 'And I must love my neighbour as much as I love myself. But… who exactly is my neighbour?'

Jesus answered him by telling the man a story about a stranger from Samaria, someone whom Jewish people would not like and would normally have no respect for.

Lord, help me to love you today with all my heart and soul and strength…

Should I help anyone who needs me?

God sees no differences between us but loves us all. We should treat others the same way.

📖 *Luke 10:30-37*

'A man was travelling from Jerusalem to Jericho,' said Jesus, 'when he was attacked and left for dead.

'A priest came by – but he walked past and would not touch him. Another holy man crossed over so he wouldn't get too close to the wounded man.

'The wounded man was sure that he would die. But then a Samaritan came along the road. The Samaritan stopped, bathed and bandaged the man's wounds, then helped him on to his own donkey. He took him to an inn and paid for the man to be looked after till he was well.

'Who do you think was a good neighbour to the man who was hurt?' asked Jesus.

The man replied, 'The one who was kind to him.'

Help me to see people the way you do, Lord, and help anyone who needs me.

I am better than you!

We should do our very best to please God and not be concerned about whether we are better, or not as good, as someone else.

📖 *Matthew 18:1-10*

The disciples saw all the things Jesus did. They listened to all the things he taught them about God. But they didn't always understand.

'Who is the greatest in the Kingdom of Heaven?' they asked him.

Jesus called a little child to join them. 'The greatest in the kingdom of heaven is someone like this child,' he said. 'A child does not worry about who is greatest but accepts what he is given simply and humbly.

'And anyone who welcomes a little child like this on my behalf welcomes me; but don't ever hurt a child like this or tempt them to do something bad – I could think of no worse thing you could do.'

Help me, Lord, to do the best I can and be the best I can be for you.

Learning to forgive

Just as God is generous in forgiving us – we should always forgive others.

 Matthew 18:21-35

'How often should I forgive someone who hurts me?' Peter asked Jesus. 'Seven times?'

'Try seventy times seven – there should be no limit at all!' Jesus replied.

'Imagine a king who is generous to someone who owes him money. The man can't pay the huge amount he owes, so he begs not to be made a slave to repay the king. The king forgives the huge debt.

'But then the man finds someone who owes him money, a much smaller amount. That man cannot pay either, but even when he begs for more time to pay, the first man sends him to prison.

'Will the king not be angry when he finds out? Should you not always be kind and generous to others because God is always kind and generous to you?'

I am sorry, Lord, when I remember hurts and don't make up quickly with others. Please give me a generous heart.

How is Jesus like a good Shepherd?

Jesus knew all about sheep and about how much they mattered to the shepherd who cared about them.

 John 10:11-15

Thank you, Jesus, that you know us by our names and each of us is special to you.

There were many sheep in the land where Jesus lived. They had funny faces and woolly coats but looked very much the same as each other to anyone who didn't know them.

But each shepherd knew their sheep and the sheep knew the shepherd's voice.

'A hired man does not feel the same way about his sheep as a shepherd,' said Jesus. 'He will run away when the wolf comes to kill them. But you are like my sheep. I am the Good Shepherd, and I would even die to take care of my sheep.'

Have you ever felt so lost that you don't think even God cares about you?

Jesus knew that God would do anything, even give his own son, to save one lost soul.

📖 *Luke 15:3-7*

Jesus told this story to explain how much God loves us.

'Imagine you own a hundred sheep,' said Jesus. 'One day you count them to find that there are only 99. Where is the missing sheep? You search everywhere for that little lost sheep – under hedgerows, over the side of cliffs, in bramble bushes – and do not rest till you have found him and can carry him home again on your shoulders!

'God's love for us is like that. He cares about everyone, especially the one that is lost and alone.'

Thank you for your love for us, Lord. Thank you that there is nowhere we can go where you can't reach us.

The huge kindness of God

Do we ever wish God was not generous but only fair?

 Matthew 20:1-15

'God's kingdom is like this,' said Jesus. 'A landowner went out early one morning to hire people to work in his vineyard. He agreed what to pay them and sent them out to work.

'At nine o'clock he hired more people; then again more at midday, at three o'clock and five o'clock in the afternoon.

'That evening he called in the workers. He paid the same amount to those who came late, as to those who came very early.

'That's not fair!' the first men said. 'Those people worked only one hour, yet you've paid them the same as us though we worked all day!'

'I wanted to be generous,' the landowner said. 'Don't be jealous if I am kind to those who worked for only a short time.'

Thank you, Lord, that you accept all who come to you, no matter what age they are.

Do you mean what you say?

God is more interested in what's in our hearts than the words we use.

 Matthew 21:28-32

'Once there was a man with two sons,' said Jesus. 'He told his older son to go out and work in the vineyard. "I don't want to go..." he told his father. But later he changed his mind and went.

'Then the father told his other son to work in the vineyard. "Of course, Father," he said. But the younger son didn't go.

'Which boy did what his father asked?'

The disciples saw that it was the first son.

'Listen, when John the Baptist showed you the right way to live, you didn't believe him or change your ways – but all the "bad" people did. In the same way, those "bad" people will be in God's kingdom first if they realize they need God – rather than those who say the right things but don't do them.'

Help me, Lord, both to say and do the right things.

Treasure in heaven

Jesus told his disciples that God will give to us all he has.

📖 *Luke 12:32-34*

'Don't be afraid for the needs of today,' said Jesus. 'God is your Father. It makes him happy to give you all he has. Sell what you have and give to those in need. You don't need treasure here on earth – be kind to others, share what you have and instead store your treasure in heaven where it is always safe. No one can steal it there and no moths can destroy it.

'So don't focus on getting more "stuff" but focus on what really matters. Look beyond what you can see now to what matters most to God.'

Help us to be kind to anyone who needs our help, Lord. Make us generous people who care most about what you want.

What does God want from us?

The prophet Micah told God's people that the answer to that was far simpler than they realized.

 *Micah 6:6-8*

'You ask how you can make up for the wrong things you have done,' said Micah. 'You ask if you should offer sacrifices to show you are sorry.

'No, no, you have it all wrong. Would it please God to have thousands of animals slaughtered or be given rivers running with olive oil? Would he be satisfied if you offered him your oldest child as a sacrifice? Would he then forgive your sins? Of course not!

'No, God has told you what he wants, and this is all it is: to love what is fair, to be just and merciful, and to walk humbly with your God.'

Lord, make us honest and fair and forgiving to others. Help us to live humbly and to see what a great God you are.

What matters most in life?

Jesus warned that the value of our lives is not measured in how rich we are.

 Luke 12:15-21

'Don't keep wishing for things you do not have,' Jesus said. 'Life is so much more important than the things money can buy.'

Then Jesus told a story. 'Once there was a rich farmer who had a very good harvest. He did so well that he had to pull down his barns and build new bigger, better barns to store all the crops he now had.

'"What a lucky man I am!" he thought. "Now I can put up my feet and relax. I can do all the things I enjoy most."

'But that night, the man died. His wealth was no good to him any more.'

Help us not to be greedy, Lord, or think only of ourselves but to share the blessings we have with others.

What happens when we do something we're ashamed of?

Jesus said God waits for us to come to him to say sorry – and welcomes us back.

 *Luke 15:11-32*

Jesus told another of his stories about a man who had two sons.

'The younger son was bored working on his father's farm. He wanted to travel and have adventures. He asked for his inheritance, left home and had a great time with his new friends, until all his money was spent.

'Suddenly his friends were gone. He was hungry and miserable. He found a job feeding pigs but was so hungry he wanted to eat the pigs' food…

'"This is silly," he realized. "I would be better off as a servant on my father's farm."

'When he was still some distance away, his father saw him and rushed to meet him. He threw his arms around him and hugged him. "Let's celebrate!" he said. "My son was lost, but now he's found!"'

Lord, thank you that you never stop loving us and welcome us back, whatever we have done.

Spending time with God

Are we sometimes too busy to stop and listen to God speaking to us?

📖 Luke 10:38-41

Jesus was very good friends with a man named Lazarus and his sisters, Martha and Mary, who lived in a village called Bethany.

One day Jesus and his disciples stopped at their house. 'Come in, come in!' said Martha. She made her guests comfortable and then hurried into the kitchen to prepare food and drinks for them all.

But while Martha was being busy in the kitchen, Mary sat with their guests and listened to all Jesus was telling them about God.

'Tell Mary to come and help me!' Martha called out to Jesus.

But Jesus shook his head. 'Mary is fine here with me,' he said. 'You mustn't be so anxious, Martha. Sometimes it's better to spend time with people while you can.'

Help us always to make time to listen to you, Lord.

Who does God welcome into his kingdom?

God invites everyone to come – but he will not force those who do not want to be there.

📖 *Luke 14:16-23*

Jesus told another story about God's kingdom.

'A man prepared a great feast and sent out many invitations. When the banquet was ready, he sent his servant to bring the guests to enjoy it. But they all began making excuses. They all had things to do that they thought were more important.

'When the man heard what had happened, he was angry. He told his servant to go into the streets and invite the poor, the homeless and those who were ill so the room would be full of those who wanted to be there.'

Thank you, Lord, that there is room for us all in your kingdom. Make us ready to come.

246

How often do we thank God?

God loves us to ask for things – but he also likes to hear our joy at his answers.

📖 *Luke 17:11-19*

Thank you, thank you, thank you, Lord.

As Jesus was walking with his disciples towards Jerusalem, they saw ten lepers standing at the edge of a village calling to Jesus to help them.

Jesus looked at them and said, 'Go to the Jewish priest and show him that you are healed!'

The men did as Jesus asked and they were indeed healed. They could hardly believe it! They showed each other their smooth, healthy skin and hurried on.

One of them, a Samaritan, came back to Jesus and fell to the ground in front of him, praising God for healing him.

Jesus smiled at him and told him to go home. But he looked sadly into the distance. Why did the others not thank God too?

What kind of person are you?

Do you think you are better than everyone else?

📖 *Luke 18:10-14*

'There were two men praying in the temple,' said Jesus. 'One was a Pharisee, a holy man, while the other was a tax collector – the sort of man everyone hated!

'The Pharisee prayed: "Thank you, God, that I am not like other people – those who cheat and lie and break your commandments. Thank you that I am generous and godly – and better than that man over there!"

'But the tax collector did not even look up. "Please, God, be kind to me, for I am not good enough to ask anything from you; I deserve nothing."

'God listened to the tax collector because he was humble but not the proud Pharisee who thought too much of himself.'

Help me never to think myself better than everyone else, Lord.

248

Can we live for ever?

Jesus told his friend Martha that people who believe in him will have eternal life.

📖 John 11:1-27

Jesus' friend Lazarus became very ill. His sisters, Mary and Martha sent a message to Jesus to come to help him.

Jesus loved his friend very much but he didn't reach the family for several days. By the time he got there, Martha came out to tell him that her brother was already dead. They had buried him four days before.

'If only you had been here, my brother would not have died,' Martha told him. 'But even now I know that it is not too late.'

'I am the resurrection and the life,' said Jesus. 'Anyone who believes in me will live, even after they have died. Everyone who believes in me will live for ever. Do you believe this, Martha?'

'Yes, Lord,' she told him. 'I have always believed you are God's Son.'

Lord, I believe in you. I am your friend. Thank you that I can live with you for ever.

Does Jesus care when we suffer?

Jesus comforted the family of his dead friend and wept with them.

📖 John 11:28-45

Martha went to fetch her sister, Mary, who was inside the house weeping and grieving for her dead brother.

Mary went to meet Jesus outside the village, followed by all the friends who had come to mourn with the sisters.

Jesus was moved by the suffering and grief of the family and friends and asked to be taken to the grave of his friend. Then Jesus also wept.

He asked them to roll aside the stone door and prayed aloud to God his father. Then he called out to Lazarus to come from the tomb.

And the dead man came out, his hands and feet bound in graveclothes and his face wrapped in a headcloth.

Many of the people there believed that Jesus was God's Son when they saw this happen. It was a miracle.

Lord, you cried with Martha and Mary even though you knew that Lazarus would live again. Thank you that you weep with us when we are grieving and suffering.

Do we make time for people?

Jesus never turned anyone away, old or young – he always had time to listen.

 Mark 10:13-16

Among the crowds of people who gathered wherever Jesus went were children. Mothers also brought them to Jesus so he could bless them. Some just followed Jesus to hear what he would say.

Jesus always had time for children. He laughed with them and told them stories. They loved to be wherever he was.

'My kingdom is made up of people like these children,' Jesus said. 'Their faith is simple. They are ready to love and trust God with all their hearts.'

Lord, help me to value other people more than things and be ready to listen when someone needs to talk.

Is there something coming between us and God?

Jesus told us to put God first and other things fall into place.

📖 Mark 10:17-25

A young man once came to Jesus and asked, 'What do I have to do to live in heaven?'

Jesus knew the man had a good heart, but he was very rich. There was something getting in the way.

'Love God more than you love your money,' Jesus answered. 'Give it away to the poor. They need it and you have more than enough.'

The man looked at Jesus sadly. He shook his head and walked slowly away. He was very rich and he knew that he could not do as Jesus asked. His money was very important to him, more important than his love for God.

Is there something in my life I should give up, Lord? Is there anything I love more than you?

When things are worrying us, Lord, help us not to be too proud or afraid to ask you for help.

What stops us asking God for help?

When the blind man asked, he was given what he asked for.

 Luke 18:35-43

As usual when Jesus was travelling through any town, the streets of Jericho were lined with people. When a blind beggar asked what all the noise was about, someone told him that Jesus was passing by.

The blind man knew that Jesus healed people. Perhaps Jesus would help him too?

'Jesus, Son of David, have mercy on me!' he shouted at the top of his voice.

'Be quiet!' people shouted back. 'Jesus is busy!' But the beggar kept trying to get Jesus' attention.

'What do you want me to do for you?' Jesus asked.

'I want to see!' the blind man said.

'Your faith has made you well,' Jesus replied. 'Go now: you can see!'

The blind beggar was overjoyed to have been given his sight. He got up and joined the people who followed Jesus.

When Zacchaeus met Jesus, his whole life changed.

What difference does knowing Jesus make to you?

📖 *Luke 19:1-10*

The streets were packed as Jesus went through Jericho. No one was going to make room for Zacchaeus, the rich tax collector. He was a cheat!

Zacchaeus wanted to see Jesus very much. He couldn't see over the heads of the crowd so he climbed a fig tree so that he could see Jesus as he passed by.

But Jesus could see Zacchaeus too. He stopped and smiled up at him. 'Zacchaeus, I'd like to visit your house today,' Jesus said.

Zacchaeus changed when he met Jesus.

'I'm going to give half my money to the poor,' he said. 'I will even pay back what I have stolen – and much more too!'

'I came to find people like Zacchaeus who need God's help,' said Jesus. 'This is why I am here.'

Show us, Lord, what needs to change in our lives because we know you and love you.

God always gives us another chance

Do we sometimes feel God will never forgive us?

📖 *1 Kings 11:42-43, 17:1*

King Solomon lived a long life, but after his death came many kings of Israel who did not love God or care about doing the good things Solomon knew God wanted.

King Ahab had broken many of God's Ten Commandments. He had married a woman named Jezebel and built a temple to her false god, Baal. Then they both worshipped the false god. God wanted to give Ahab a chance to change. So God sent the prophet Elijah to warn him.

'God is the only true and living God,' said Elijah. 'But you worship gods of wood and stone who can do nothing. Now God has decided that unless you change your ways and keep his commandments, he will send no more rain.'

Thank you, Lord, that you always give us a chance to change; that you are always ready to forgive.

God takes cares of his children

Can you think of times when God has helped you?

 1 Kings 17:2-6

King Ahab was very angry when he heard God's message.

God told Elijah to leave the king and go to hide in a ravine east of the River Jordan where he could get water from a brook to drink. Then God sent ravens to Elijah with bread and meat each morning and with bread and meat each evening.

God took care of Elijah.

But no rain fell on the earth. The sun beat down and the earth was dry and parched. Eventually even the brook dried up.

Then God sent Elijah to a town called Zarephath where he said a godly widow would help him and give him food.

You have given us so much, Lord, and always been there when we needed your help.

Taking God at his word

How hard is it for us to take a step of faith when it really matters?

📖 1 Kings 17:10-16

Elijah walked in the hot sun to Zarephath and met the widow, gathering sticks. Elijah was very thirsty.

'Will you help me?' he asked. 'Could you bring me some water… and a piece of bread?'

'I have none,' she answered, 'just a little flour and a drop of oil. I am about to make bread for our last meal. Then my son and I will die.'

'Trust God,' said Elijah. 'Share what you have with me now. God has promised that your flour will not run out, nor your jug of oil run dry.'

The widow baked the bread for Elijah and there was enough flour and oil for more bread, just as he had said. God provided for Elijah and the widow's family until rain fell once more upon the earth.

Help us to be kind to others even when we don't have much ourselves.

It's your fault!

Do we blame others when we are in the wrong?

 1 Kings 18:1-19

Nearly three years had passed. Still it had not rained.

'Go back to see Ahab,' God said to Elijah. 'I will send rain once more.'

On his way back, Elijah met another prophet, Obadiah, who had hidden many other prophets to protect them from the angry Queen Jezebel. Obadiah arranged the meeting with King Ahab.

'Here you are, you troublemaker!' said King Ahab.

'Me?' Elijah replied. 'No, you are the troublemaker. This is all because of you and your father's family. You knew what God wanted of you – but you have chosen to worship gods of wood and stone. Come now with all the prophets who serve the god Baal – and meet me on Mount Carmel. Then we will see who is the true and living God.'

Lord, help us to own up to our mistakes and wrongdoings and ask you to forgive us.

Lord, help us not to be swayed by fashion or the opinions of others but to seek for the truth – and follow it with all our hearts.

Choose whom you will worship!

Knowing God requires a response on our part.

 1 Kings 18:20-29

King Ahab brought all the false prophets together on Mount Carmel along with all the people he ruled.

Then Elijah spoke to the Israelites. 'It is time to choose,' he said. 'Who is the true and living God? If the Lord is God, then follow him. But if Baal is god, follow him.'

Elijah challenged the prophets of Baal to prepare a sacrifice to their god while he did the same.

'Pray to your god and I will pray to mine to send down fire on the altar.'

The prophets made their altar and prayed and danced and danced and prayed. But there was no answer. Nothing happened at all.

'Is your god too busy to answer?' said Elijah. 'Is he on holiday – or maybe he's asleep? Shout louder!'

But still there was no answer.

God is great!

Elijah did not doubt that God was real. He was sure he could be trusted.

 1 Kings 18:30-39

Then Elijah built his altar and dug a small trench around it. He asked the people to fill four jars of water.

'Pour the water over the wood and the sacrifice until everything is soaking wet.'

The water flowed over Elijah's altar until it filled the trench. Surely no fire could burn up Elijah's sacrifice now?

Then Elijah prayed. 'Lord, show these people that you alone are God. Turn their hearts back to you so they will know they are your special people. Answer me and light up this altar with fire.'

Suddenly fire fell from heaven and burned the wet wood on the altar – and even dried up the water in the trench. God had answered Elijah and shown all the people that he was the true and living God.

The people knelt down and worshipped him. 'The Lord – he is God! The Lord – he is God!' they said.

Lord, may our lives show that we believe in you and that we trust you to act when we call on you.

260

Have you ever felt no one understands you?

Elijah was human and he felt overwhelmed.

 1 Kings 19:1-16

Queen Jezebel was now even more keen to take revenge on God's prophet.

Elijah ran for his life!

He travelled to Mount Horeb and found a cave in which to shelter. But he was exhausted. He was lonely.

'What are you doing here?' God asked him.

'I have done all you asked me to!' said Elijah. 'But still people are trying to kill me!'

'Stand on the mountain, Elijah. I am going to pass by.'

Then Elijah heard a powerful wind shatter rocks around him. But God was not in the wind. The ground cracked under him. But God was not in the earthquake. Fire roared around him, but God was not in the fire. Then Elijah heard a gentle whisper… And God told Elijah to go to Elisha who would help him with his work.

Thank you, Lord, that you understand when we cannot cope any more – and you comfort and help us.

Do you respect those older than you?

Elisha took care of Elijah until the end.

📖 *1 Kings 19:19-21, 2 Kings 2:1-11*

Elijah went to find Elisha, who said goodbye to his parents and then left home to help Elijah serve God.

Elijah was now an old man. 'Stay here,' he told Elisha one day. 'I must go on alone. God is sending me to Bethel. But Elisha went with him.

'Stay here,' Elijah told Elisha. 'God is sending me to Jericho. But Elisha went with him.

'Stay here,' Elijah said a third time. 'God is sending me to the Jordan. But Elisha went with him. He knew that soon Elijah would go to be with God.

When they reached the River Jordan Elijah divided the water for them to cross. Then a chariot of fire carried Elijah away to heaven in a whirlwind.

Elijah had gone and God blessed Elisha with his power. Now God would speak through him.

Lord, help us to respect and take care of those who need our care and support.

262

Lord, take the boundaries away from our love for others so that we are kind to anyone who needs our help.

Are there limits to our kindness to others?

The servant girl did not hold a grudge but offered help to the man who made her his prisoner.

 2 Kings 5:1-10

Naaman was a proud man, a much-valued commander of the King of Aram's army. He was a great soldier and had won many victories in battle; but Naaman was not happy because he suffered from leprosy, an infectious disease which destroyed the nerves in his skin.

An Israelite girl had been taken prisoner and made to work as a servant in Naaman's house.

'I wish my master would visit the prophet Elisha in the land of my home,' she whispered to her mistress. 'I am sure that God could cure him of his leprosy.'

Carrying a letter from the king of Aram, Naaman went to the king of Israel asking for a cure, taking with him generous gifts of gold, silver and fine clothes.

The king of Israel was not a godly man. He panicked. 'How can I do that?' he shouted. 'Am I God?! This is an excuse to make war upon me!'

Do we try to earn God's mercy?

Naaman brought gifts – but God's mercy is freely given to all.

 2 Kings 5:9-15

The king of Israel did not know God – but Elisha did. He told the king to send Naaman to him.

Naaman stopped outside Elisha's door with his gifts, his horses and his chariots. But Elisha did not go out to see him. Instead he sent his servant with a message.

'Go and wash seven times in the River Jordan and you will be healed.'

Naaman was a proud man and he expected more from Elisha. And why should he wash in the dirty River Jordan when there were better rivers in Aram! He was very angry. But Naaman's servant encouraged him.

'If the prophet had asked you to do something difficult, you would have done it. Why not see if this will heal you?'

So Naaman washed seven times – and his skin was whole and new again.

'Now I know that there is no God in all the world except the God of Israel,' he said.

Lord, forgive our pride and help us always to be willing to accept help, both from you and from others.

Who does God choose to serve him?

God chooses the old and the young; men and women and children; people who have many gifts and ordinary people, just like us.

 Jeremiah 1:1-9

Jeremiah was still very young when God chose him to be his prophet.

'I had plans for you, Jeremiah, even before you were born,' said God. 'I knew you already and had decided what I wanted you to do.'

'But surely I am too young,' said Jeremiah. 'I won't know what to say.'

The people had again forgotten God's commandments. They worshipped false gods – again! God needed a messenger to warn them to come back to him and seek his help.

'You are not too young,' God answered, 'because I will be there to guide and help you. I will give you the words to say. Trust me, Jeremiah. Go to the people with the words I will give you.'

Thank you, Lord, that anyone can serve you if they are willing. Thank you that you can use even me.

God knows us

David believed God knew everything about him and still loved him.

📖 *Psalm 139:1-16*

'Lord God, you have seen my heart and know not only what I think but why I do the things I do. You know everything about me. You know where I am and what I am doing; you guide me and you bless me. You know what I am going to say before I say it.

'There is no place I can go where your love can't reach me; no dark place where I might be afraid. It's amazing! It's a wonderful fact that even if I feel I am lost, I can never be lost to you. You are always there.

'You put me together in my mother's womb – you created every part of me with all my body's complex workings. You saw what kind of person I would be before I was born and planned each day of my life before I began to breathe.'

How precious it is, Lord, to realize that I am never far from your thoughts! When I come to you for help, you know just who I am and you know what I need.

Something beautiful for God

God does not give up on us when we let him down.

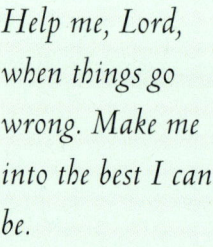 *Jeremiah 18:1-6*

One of the first things God asked Jeremiah to do was to visit the potter's house.

Jeremiah watched as the potter's wheel spun around and around. First the clay made a round useful pot but then it wobbled and became a strange shape. It was good for nothing.

The potter took the clay and reshaped it so it was not wasted but turned into something new. It became beautiful in the hands of the potter.

Jeremiah saw that God was like the potter and his people were like the clay. Even when things went wrong, God could change his people into something better; God could make something beautiful out of something bad.

Help me, Lord, when things go wrong. Make me into the best I can be.

How do we react when we hear God's words?

The Bible is full of examples of people who wouldn't listen when God spoke.

 Jeremiah 36:1-26

God gave his message of warning to Jeremiah and Jeremiah's friend Baruch wrote it down on a long scroll. Baruch then went to the temple to read it to the people.

When people heard it, they were anxious. They took it seriously. They thought it was so important that King Jehoiakim should hear it too.

King Jehoiakim was in the winter palace sitting in front of a fire. He let the words on the scroll be read aloud but he didn't want to listen to God. As each part of the scroll was read out to him, the king sliced off that part of the scroll and threw it into the fire.

When the whole scroll was burned, he sent people to arrest Jeremiah and Baruch. But they had hidden themselves away!

Then Jeremiah sat down with Baruch… and began writing down God's words all over again.

Open our ears to listen, Lord. Open our hearts to obey.

Dark days, dark nights

We all have times when God seems far away. Jeremiah must have felt God had deserted him.

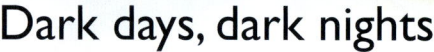 *Jeremiah 37:1-20*

King Zedekiah became king in Jerusalem. Neither he nor his officials listened to Jeremiah either.

'Tell him the Egyptians will not help him,' said God. 'The Babylonians will attack the city. They will not rest until they have captured the people and the city is in flames.'

While the armies were fighting on the borders, Jeremiah left the city to look at a piece of land he owned.

'Where are you going?' demanded the captain of the guard. 'You are a deserter!'

Jeremiah was beaten and put into a dark cell in a dungeon. Day after day Jeremiah lived in the dungeon not knowing what would happen next. Then one day the king had him brought into the palace.

'Do you have a message from God?' he asked.

'God told me the Babylonians will come and capture you,' said Jeremiah. 'But please don't send me back to that dark cell or I will die!'

Help us to trust you, Lord, when there seems to be no hope.

Do we have a sense of purpose?

Jeremiah was dedicated to serving God whatever the cost.

 *Jeremiah 37:21 – 38:6*

The king had Jeremiah moved to the palace courtyard which was much better than his dark cell. But Jeremiah had been given a message from God himself and he could not keep quiet. He told anyone who would listen that they should surrender to the Babylonians — or they would die.

When the king's officials heard him, they were very angry.

'This man is upsetting everyone!' they said.

They threw Jeremiah into an empty well and left him there to die. Jeremiah sank deep into the mud at the bottom. It was worse than his dark cell.

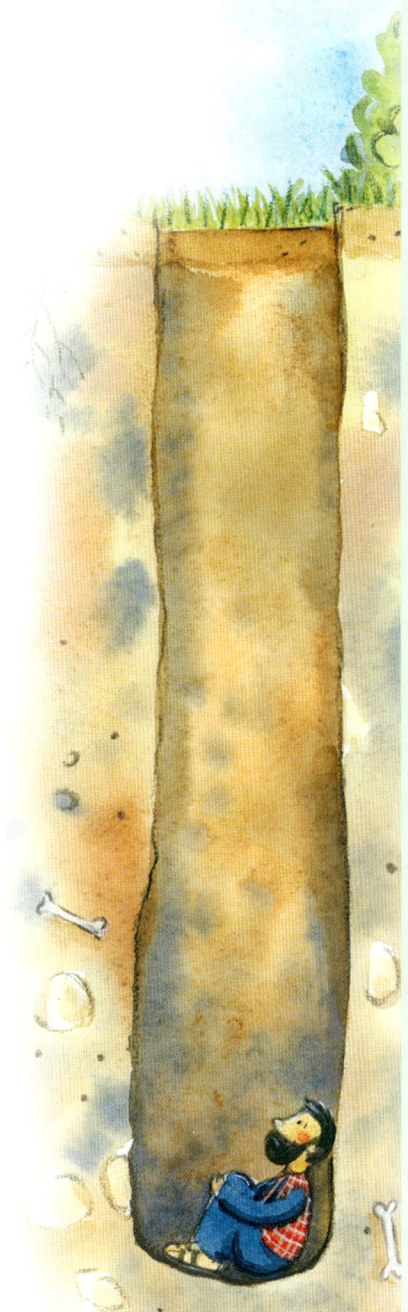

Help us to take the message of your love to everyone we meet today — and every day.

270 Do we stand up for those with no voice?

Jeremiah's friend was brave enough to plead with the king to help him.

📖 Jeremiah 38:7-13

One of Jeremiah's friends saw how miserable he was in the well and went to see the king.

'My Lord the king, your men have done terrible things to Jeremiah. He will starve to death if you leave him in that well! Please do something to save him – he doesn't deserve to be treated like this.'

The king listened. They threw some old clothes down to Jeremiah for him to put under his arms so the ropes would not cut and burn him. Then thirty men pulled Jeremiah out of the well. He was safe.

Lord, help us to stand up for others when they are being badly treated.

No limits

Jeremiah's job had not been easy; but he had done his job faithfully.

📖 *Jeremiah 38:17 – 40:6*

When the king saw Jeremiah again he demanded good news.

'I can only tell you what God tells me,' he said. 'You must surrender to the Babylonians. Do this and you will live.'

But the king would not trust God. When the Babylonians captured Jerusalem, they broke down the walls of Jerusalem and burned the palace to the ground; they stole the precious things from Solomon's temple and destroyed the beautiful building. They killed the king's sons and blinded him before taking him and many others away in chains.

The Babylonian commander came looking for Jeremiah.

'Your God said all this would happen,' he said, 'because no one would listen to him. But you have done nothing wrong, Jeremiah. You are free. You can come with me or you can stay here.'

Jeremiah chose to stay behind. There were many poor people there who needed his help.

Make us willing to do the hard things for you, Lord, not just those that bring rewards. Help us not to set limits on what we will do for you.

272

Are we good at making the best of a bad situation?

Even when captive in a foreign land, Daniel wanted to keep God's laws.

📖 *Daniel 1:1-16*

Daniel, Shadrach, Meshach and Abednego were well educated young men taken as captives from Jerusalem. The king in Babylon wanted them to be trained to work for him in the palace.

They were surprised that they were treated very well. At first they were offered meat and wine from the king's table to eat but Daniel knew that it had been offered first to the pretend gods the Babylonians worshipped. He did not want to break God's commandments so he asked if they could have vegetables and water instead.

The man in charge of them was worried. What if they became ill? The king would surely blame him! But he agreed to let them try the diet for ten days. At the end of that time they looked healthier than those eating the king's food and they were allowed to continue.

Help us, Lord, to behave as if we love you wherever we are and whatever happens to us.

Does accepting God's blessings mean we don't have to try?

Daniel and his friends worked hard even when they were prisoners.

📖 *Daniel 1:17-21*

God blessed the four young men while they were in Babylon. They worked hard and God blessed them so that after their training was completed, they knew more than anyone else in Babylon. God also gave Daniel the gift of being able to understand dreams.

All the men who had been trained were brought before the king and tested. The king was impressed with them all but particularly with Daniel, Shadrach, Meshach and Abednego. He made them four of his trusted advisers. He preferred them and their advice to all the other men in his kingdom.

Lord,. whatever we have to do, help us to do our best in eveery situation.

Dreams and visions

God had sent a dream to the king – but he had also sent him a man who could help him understand it.

Daniel 2:1-12

Lord, help us to come to you when things happen that we don't understand.

When Nebuchadnezzar had been king for more than a year, he had a terrible nightmare. He woke up very frightened and called all his advisers. But he couldn't remember what he had dreamed about!

'Tell me what I dreamed last night!' he demanded. 'I know something terrible is going to happen!'

'Tell us the dream and we will tell you what it means,' said his advisers.

'I can't!' said the king, even more distressed. 'I can't remember! But if you can't help me, I will have every last one of you killed!'

The magicians trembled. They knew they couldn't. 'But there is no man alive who can do this!' they said. 'Only God knows what dreams men have.'

The king was very angry. 'Then prepare to die!' he said.

Why does God give us gifts?

God gives us what we need so we can help others.

📖 *Daniel 2:12-23*

Daniel and his friends had not been with the other advisers that night but they knew all about what had happened when men came to arrest them.

Then Daniel went to see the king.

'Give me a little more time,' he said,' and I will tell you what you dreamed and what it means.'

Then Daniel went to his three friends and together they prayed as they had never prayed before, asking God to show them the mystery of what the king had dreamed.

That night God answered their prayers and Daniel praised God. 'You know everything, Lord, and you are good and kind to tell us now what no man could ever know. Thank you!'

Then Daniel went to see King Nebuchadnezzar.

Lord, help us to come to you with all our fears and problems. I want to tell you about some of them now...

How do we feel when God answers our prayers?

Are we amazed? Do we thank him and tell him how great he is?

 Daniel 2:26-47

'Is it true? Can you tell me what I dreamed?' the king asked Daniel.

'No wise man or magician on earth can tell you your dream,' Daniel replied, 'but there is a God in heaven and he has shown it to me.

'You saw a huge statue hit by a rock and smashed into a million pieces. Then the rock became a great mountain.

'This is a warning! Now you are a great king in control of a great nation, but one day, others will come and destroy you and you will have no power. Finally, God's kingdom will come, and all the nations on earth will know that God alone is king.'

Then the king thanked Daniel. 'Your God really is great – and can reveal hidden mysteries,' he said.

Lord, thank you that even though you know us completely – even what we are thinking and feeling – you still love us.

Do we take seriously what God tells us?

It's one thing to know what we should do and quite another to actually do it.

 *Daniel 2:48 – 3:23*

King Nebuchadnezzar gave Daniel and his three friends important jobs in his kingdom. But the king soon forgot God's warning. He made a huge golden statue of himself like the one in his dream. People could see it for miles around.

'Everyone in the kingdom must bow down and worship my statue as soon as they hear music!' he said.

But Shadrach, Meshach and Abednego would worship only God. They would not bow down.

The three men were brought before the king.

'Is this true?' he asked. 'I will give you one more chance.'

'Don't worry about us,' they answered. 'Our God is able to save us whatever you do to us. But even if he doesn't, we will not worship your statue.'

So they were thrown into a fiery furnace.

Dear God, help us to listen to what we should do and then be willing to obey and do the right thing.

Do we believe God can work miracles?

Shadrach, Meshach and Abednego knew God could save them but they did not expect him to.

 Daniel 3:24-28

Nebuchadnezzar watched the three men fall into the hot flames – but then he stood back in amazement.

'Did we not throw three men into the fire? How can it be that I can see four men walking about in the flames? They don't even seem to be hurt!'

Nebuchadnezzar came as close as he could to the flaming furnace and shouted to the men.

'Shadrach, Meshach and Abednego, come out! Come here!'

And to everyone's amazement, the men stepped out of the fire, untouched by the flames, not even smelling a little like smoke.

'We must all praise your God, the God of Shadrach, Meshach and Abednego,' said the king, 'for he sent an angel to keep his servants safe from the fire. No other god can do as your God can.'

Help us, Lord, to obey you because it's the right thing to do but not to demand miracles from you to suit ourselves.

How much do we value sacred things?

While things in themselves may not be important, we should be in awe of the living God.

 Daniel 5:1-6

When King Nebuchadnezzar died, his son Belshazzar became king.

Daniel was now an old man and no one wanted him at court. Belshazzar did not even know Daniel.

Then one day the king threw a party for a thousand of the most important people in Babylon. He used the beautiful gold and silver goblets that his father had stolen from the temple in Jerusalem, and praised the gods he believed in, of gold and silver, wood and stone.

Suddenly the king's face went pale with fear. On the wall in front of him words appeared, written by the hand of an invisible man. No one could believe what was happening! The event had turned from a celebration into a horrible nightmare.

Lord, we know we are your children, loved and cared for. Help us nonetheless to respect you as the holy God, creator of all the world.

If God tested us, what would he find?

The king was proud and greedy and had no time for the living God. He did not pass the test.

 Daniel 5:7-31

The king did not know the meaning of the words on the wall. None of the king's magicians knew what the message said either. The king became even more frightened.

When the king's mother heard what had happened she rushed into the room.

'Don't be afraid,' she said. 'When your father was king he trusted a man who understood the mind of God. He will help you. His name is Daniel.'

So they found Daniel and he came to explain the meaning of the words on the wall.

'God has counted the days you will be king,' Daniel read. 'They are over! God has tested you, and you have not passed the test. Now your kingdom will be given to the Medes and the Persians.'

Lord, help us to examine our lives – and show us where we could do better.

Have you ever been jealous of what someone else has?

Jealousy is destructive, often leading to bitterness, hatred and a desire to hurt someone else.

📖 *Daniel 5:30 – 6:4*

Belshazzar ordered great honours to be given to Daniel because of his help. Daniel was given clothes made of expensive purple fabric and a gold chain to wear around his neck. He was proclaimed the third highest ruler in the kingdom…

All that Daniel had said came true. That very night, Belshazzar was killed and Darius the Mede became king. Then King Darius appointed Daniel as one of many men who would help to rule his kingdom.

He was so pleased with everything Daniel did that he gave him even more power… So Daniel had a great friend – but he also made plenty of enemies, men who were jealous of the power he had been given.

Help us, Lord, to be happy for others when they succeed, and not to let small sins become much greater sins.

Could you be flattered into making a bad choice?

It was King Darius' vanity that made him pass a new law, thinking he was as great as God.

📖 *Daniel 6:4-15*

The men who were jealous of Daniel began to plot. They wanted to find a way to get Daniel into trouble with the king. But Daniel was a good man; they could find nothing wrong – except his love for God.

They began to form a clever plan. They told King Darius how great he was. They persuaded him to pass a new law. If someone prayed to anyone but him, that person would be thrown into a den of lions!

What would Daniel do? Daniel did what he did every day. He went home and prayed to God. His enemies' plot had worked! Daniel had broken the new law.

King Darius did not want to hurt Daniel, but he knew that the law could not be changed. He also realized he had been tricked.

Forgive us, Lord, when we think too highly of ourselves and become proud and thoughtless.

Do you think God can be trusted?

Daniel trusted God with his life; but the king was afraid of what might happen next.

 *Daniel 6:16-28*

Daniel was marched away and thrown into a den of lions. The door was locked tight.

King Darius shouted through the door, 'May your God save you, Daniel!'

The king was so worried that he could not eat that evening and he could not sleep that night. In the morning he hurried to the lions' den.

'Has your God been able to save you from the lions, Daniel?' he called through the door.

Then a voice came from inside the lions' den.

'God sent his angel to shut the lions' mouths,' said Daniel. 'The lions have not hurt me at all.'

King Darius released Daniel from the den and issued a new law. 'From now on, all people should respect Daniel's God, because he alone has the power to save, even from the mouths of lions.'

Our lions may not have teeth and claws, but there are still things in our lives that make us afraid. Help us, Lord, to name them and trust you to help us.

Can God work through people who don't share our faith?

284

God answers our prayers to make good things happen.

📖 Nehemiah 1:2-11

Lord, thank you for listening when we pray with humble hearts.

Artaxerxes was the king of Babylon. His cupbearer was Nehemiah, one of the Jewish exiles.

One day some of the Jews came from Jerusalem with news about the people who had returned to live there. It made Nehemiah very sad to hear that the place he had once called home was in ruins. He wept when he heard the news.

Then Nehemiah prayed to God. 'Lord, you are great and awesome – there is no one else like you. Your people have disappointed you but I know you still love them. Please help me now as I talk to the king. Make him listen kindly so that your people can return to Jerusalem and make it their home once more.'

Learning to wait…

Nehemiah prayed for a long time, waiting for God to guide him.

📖 Nehemiah 2:1-8

Four months later, the king noticed how sad his cupbearer looked.

'What's wrong, Nehemiah?' he asked.

Then Nehemiah told him about the city that used to be his home – that the gates had been burned down and the walls were still in ruins.

Nehemiah prayed again silently before asking, 'Would you allow me to go home to Jerusalem and rebuild the walls and gates?'

God was very good to Nehemiah.

'How long would you be gone?' said the king.

Artaxerxes not only said Nehemiah could go, he sent him with special letters so he could travel safely and buy wood to do the work!

Help us to keep praying and to wait for the right time to act.

Do you pray for your leaders?

Good leaders not only listen to God, but encourage others to trust him and to work well together.

 Nehemiah 2:9 – 6:19

Nehemiah went to Jerusalem and planned what could be done. He encouraged the people there, telling them all how God had answered his prayers. The people suddenly realized that things could change. They believed that God would help them.

They worked hard with Nehemiah to repair the walls of Jerusalem and built new city gates.

When their enemies made things difficult for them, Nehemiah reminded them that God was on their side – this was also God's plan. When they argued among themselves and treated each other unfairly, Nehemiah challenged them to behave as God wanted them to – and encouraged them to live together as God's people, brothers and sisters.

Together they fixed the ruined walls of Jerusalem in only fifty-two days!

Lord, guide our leaders and speak through them so that we can work together for the good of all.

What is worship?

We need to be sorry for the bad things we have done, but also thank God for his blessings and celebrate his love for us.

📖 Nehemiah 8:1-12, 13:6

As the people of Jerusalem came together inside the newly-built walls, Ezra, the priest, read to them the laws God had given to Moses. He reminded the people of God's love for them.

They wept when they realized how they had disappointed God but Ezra and Nehemiah encouraged them to eat together and celebrate how God had blessed them and all he had done for them – and to help any who were in need on this special day.

Then they thanked him for bringing them home. The Israelites tried to return to the laws and customs their ancestors had long forgotten – and to ask God's forgiveness when they made mistakes.

Eventually Nehemiah went back to work for King Artaxerxes as he had promised.

Lord, you are great but also kind. Thank you for all your blessings – and please forgive me for the bad things I have done.

288

What will happen at the end of time?

Jesus told his friends that what they do in life will be taken into account.

📖 *Matthew 25:31-34*

'One day God will judge everyone according to how they have lived,' Jesus told his disciples. 'The good people will be separated from the bad.

'"You have done well," God will say to some. "When I was hungry, you gave me food. When I needed clothes, you shared yours with me. When I was in prison or in hospital, you visited me."

'The good people will ask, "But when did we do these things?"

'God will answer, "Whenever you were kind to someone who needed help, you did it for me."'

Let us treat everyone we meet as an opportunity to show our love.

What will make God disappointed with us?

Jesus said the way we behave to those in most need reflects who we are.

📖 *Matthew 25:35-46*

Jesus said, 'God will say to the other group of people, "Go! You would not help when I was cold and hungry or needed a drink of water; you did not visit me when I was sad in prison and lonely in hospital."

'"But tell us – when did we fail to help you?" they will say. "When did we not do these things?"

'He will answer, "Whenever you saw someone who needed help and only had time for yourselves, then you were turning your back not just on them, but on me."'

Help us to see every person in need as an opportunity to show how much we love you, Lord.

290

Help us not to be quick to judge the actions of others, Lord.

How do the things we say and do show what we are really like?

Mary showed her love and devotion; Judas showed his heart was not in the right place.

 John 12:1-8

When Jesus went to visit his friends, Lazarus, Martha and Mary, he had a surprise.

The men were sitting around the table when Mary came in with a bottle of expensive perfume. Mary knelt by Jesus' feet and washed them with the perfume. The whole room was filled with the wonderful scent. Then she used her long, dark hair to dry Jesus' feet.

'What a waste!' grumbled Judas. 'We could have sold the perfume and given the money to the poor!'

But Jesus shook his head and smiled at Mary. 'No, I will not be here much longer. Mary has done something kind and generous to show her love for me.'

Are we more likely to follow a great hero or someone who is good and kind?

Jesus was not the king people expected and some did not welcome him.

John 12:12-19

It was time to prepare for the Passover Feast. Jesus asked his disciples to borrow a donkey so that he could ride into Jerusalem.

When the people saw him, they remembered that long ago, a prophet had written that their king would ride on a donkey, not a war horse. Soon they were waving branches from palm trees and cheering. They laid a path of cloaks for the donkey to ride on.

God bless Jesus! they shouted! 'Here comes King Jesus!'

'Hooray for Jesus, our king!'

The religious leaders frowned and muttered. They didn't like it. They didn't like it at all.

Help us to welcome you into our lives as Lord and King.

292

Real religion – or just for show?

Jesus challenged not just people's actions but their motives.

 Mark 11:15-18

Jesus went to the temple in Jerusalem to pray.

He was shocked when he saw all the buying and selling – many people were selling animals for offerings. But much worse, he saw that the money-changers were cheating the visitors, making money out of their desire to worship God.

'God's house is a place for love and kindness,' said Jesus. 'People come here to pray and ask God to bless them.' Then he turned over their tables. 'It's not a place for cheating and stealing!' he said.

Some of the religious leaders were watching. There was chaos. They were very angry.

'This cannot go on,' they whispered to each other. 'We must find a way to stop Jesus – for ever.'

Lord, may our motives be good in all that we do. Create in us a pure heart.

How much are we prepared to give back to God?

When we love God with all our hearts, we hold nothing back.

 Mark 12:41-44

While Jesus and his friends were in the courtyard of the temple, Jesus watched as people came and put money into the collection boxes.

Some of the people were rich and gave large amounts of money. Then a poor widow came. She dropped in two small coins.

'Look how much that woman loves God,' Jesus said to his friends. 'That woman has given two copper coins for God's work. She has very little but her gift was the most generous. The rich gave generously but had plenty left over for themselves; the woman gave God everything that she had.'

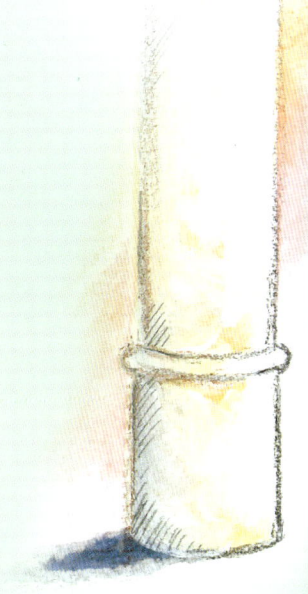

Teach us to be generous with everything you have given to us, Lord.

294

Lord, help us to be loyal followers, faithful to the end.

When friends let you down…

When have we not acted as Jesus would have wanted?

📖 *Matthew 26:3-5, 14-16*

The priests and religious leaders were angry.

'Jesus must go!' they said. 'He cannot continue teaching people about God. People won't listen to us any more.'

But they were also afraid. Everyone loved Jesus. They knew there would be a riot if they tried to arrest him. They needed one of his friends to betray him so they could do it secretly…

Jesus knew they were plotting. He told his friends that he would not be with them much longer.

Then Judas Iscariot, one of the twelve men who had been with Jesus since the beginning, went to the chief priests and asked how much they would give him if he were to betray Jesus.

They gave him thirty silver coins.

From that moment Judas looked for an opportunity to tell them where Jesus would be when the crowds were not there with him.

The servant king

Jesus led by example, being willing to take the place of a servant to show love for others.

📖 *John 13:5-20*

When the time came to celebrate together the Passover Feast, Jesus and his disciples met in the upstairs room of a house in Jerusalem.

Before they began to eat, Jesus filled a basin with water and began to wash his friends' dusty feet, drying them with the towel he had wrapped around his waist. It was usually the job of a servant and the disciples were surprised.

'No, stop! You shouldn't be doing this for us,' Peter protested.

'Follow my example,' Jesus insisted. 'If I can do this for you, you can take care of each other in the same way. Don't argue about who is the most important among you. Instead learn to do things for others that are kind and good and the world will know that you love me.'

Help us to be happy to be the ones who serve rather than those who are served by others.

Could I be the one who betrays Jesus?

When other things become more important than our love for God, we are all capable of letting Jesus down.

 John 13:21-30

As they sat at the table, Jesus was surrounded by his twelve disciples for the last time.

'You are all my friends,' he said, 'but I know that one of you will soon betray me to my enemies.'

The disciples looked at each other. They had all seen the people Jesus had healed. They had heard the stories Jesus had told them about God's love. Who could do such a thing?

'Who is it, Lord?' they asked. 'Surely not me!'

Judas looked away nervously.

Jesus turned to Judas and said, 'Do what you have to do now, but go quickly.'

The other disciples thought that Judas was going to give money to the poor. Thirty silver coins jingled in his pocket. . .

When we do things that let you down, we are so sorry, Lord. Forgive me for. . .

Is there room for everyone in heaven?

Jesus told his friends that there was plenty of room for anyone who came to him.

 *John 14:1-7*

'Don't be afraid,' said Jesus. 'Trust me to take care of you. There is plenty of room where my Father lives, places which will become your homes. I am going to prepare them so they are ready for you when the time comes. Then I will come and take you with me, and you will be with me all the time. Trust me. You know where I am going and how to get there.'

'But we don't know,' Thomas said. 'How can we know the way?'

'I am the way, the truth and the life,' said Jesus. 'Anyone who wants to be with God can come to me. If you know me, you already know God and are with God.'

Thank you that we don't need to be afraid to die, Lord. You will lead us by the hand and show us the way. You will always be there with us.

298

How can we do things that really matter?

We can let Jesus be part of our lives.

 John 15:1-16, 26-27

'I am the true vine,' said Jesus to his friends, 'and my father is the gardener. He cuts away the dead wood and prunes the branches so they produce even more fruit.

'We are part of each other; we need each other – just as a branch of the vine no longer bears fruit if it is cut off from the stem.

'If you let me live in you and become part of your life, you will be fruitful, and do the things that have real value in life.

'I love you even as God the Father loves me. Love each other too even to the point of dying for each other if necessary.

'You are my friends; I chose you and have work for you to do in the world.

'Soon I will send the Holy Spirit to you, and he will help you understand everything about me that you don't yet know. Share that knowledge with everyone you know.'

Lord, I want you in my life. I want to do things that really matter!

What difference does the Holy Spirit make?

He helps us to fight against our natural desires to do the wrong thing.

 Galatians 5:16-26

'Follow the Holy Spirit's instructions,' Paul told his friends in Galatia. 'He will tell you where to go and what to do.

'If we follow his guidance and let him control our lives, he will help us to love others and see the good in them, show us the joy of knowing Jesus, and help us to be at peace with other people; we will be patient with others, kind and gentle, good and faithful and we will know how to show self-control.

'It will be as if we have nailed our bad thoughts and actions to Jesus' cross and crucified them there.

'So live, guided by the Holy Spirit's power. Follow his leading in everything you do.'

Lord, let my life by guided by the Holy Spirit, day by day.

300

'Remember me'

When we take part in a service of Holy Communion, do we remember what Jesus did for us?

 Luke 22:14-20, 39

As Jesus sat with his friends to eat, he knew that this would be his last meal before his death. He knew that Judas was even now with his enemies; soon they would come to arrest him.

Jesus knew that his friends did not understand that something very bad was going to happen soon. In just a few hours he would be taken away from them and terrible things would happen.

Jesus broke some bread and shared it with them. 'Eat this,' he said. 'This is my body which is broken for you.' Then Jesus took a cup of wine and said, 'Drink this. This is my blood which will be spilled for you. When you do this again, remember me.'

The mood was quiet and thoughtful. What did Jesus mean?

They sang a hymn together and followed Jesus as he went to pray.

Teach us what your sacrifice meant, Lord. Help us to be thankful.

Don't think of yourselves!

The apostle Paul wrote to the church in Corinth about the way they celebrated the Holy Communion together.

 1 Corinthians 11:17-31

'Have you forgotten why we celebrate Holy Communion?

'When you come together, do you spend your time arguing with each other? Do you divide yourself into groups who hold grudges against each other? Or do you think you are having a dinner party where some are greedy and forget to share while others drink far too much?

'You know what you are supposed to do… thank God for the bread you eat. Share it among you and remember why Jesus died. Thank God for the wine you drink. Share it between you and remember that Jesus' blood was shed for you. Every time you do this you are telling the story again of what happened when Jesus shared his last supper with his friends. Keep doing this until Jesus comes to us again.

'Prepare yourself properly before you come to take communion. Ask God to forgive your sins. Think about what Jesus did for you and be thankful.'

Help us not to take your death for us for granted, Lord. Let us experience it new every time we go to a communion service so we remember what you did for us.

Jesus' struggle

Jesus gave up his life willingly for us – but it was not easy.

📖 *Matthew 26:36-41*

Jesus led eleven of his disciples in the moonlight to a garden called Gethsemane on the Mount of Olives.

'I feel sad and lonely tonight,' Jesus said to Peter, James and John. 'Stay close by; pray for me.'

Then Jesus went a little further and prayed.

'Father God, I know that there is much suffering to come. I know that soon I must die. But please, if there is any other way to save the people that you love, the people that I love, help me now. If not, then I want to do whatever you want. Please help me to be brave.'

But when Jesus went back to Peter, James and John, he found that they had fallen asleep! Jesus felt even more alone.

'Could you not pray with me even for an hour?' he asked them. 'Please keep watch and pray.'

When people ask us to pray for them, help us to take it seriously and bring their needs to you as if we love them as much as we love ourselves.

The kiss of betrayal

Do you know how it feels when someone you love turns against you?

📖 Matthew 26:42-50

Clouds were moving across the moon. Jesus knelt and prayed again.

'Please, help me now, Father. Give me the strength to do what you want me to do.'

Again Jesus returned to his friends to find them asleep. Jesus woke them and went to pray a third time. But soon he heard sounds in the trees; he saw the lights of torches.

Suddenly a band of men armed with swords and clubs sent by the religious leaders were coming towards them. And there, right at the front, coming to greet Jesus with a kiss – was Judas. It was not the kiss of friendship – Judas was giving a sign so the men would know whom to arrest.

'I know why you are here,' Jesus said to Judas. 'I am ready.'

Help us, Lord, to be loyal friends to others – and to remain your faithful followers whatever happens.

True friends?

What would you do if someone you love was in trouble?

 Matthew 26:57-68

When Jesus was arrested, the disciples were so afraid they ran away. But Peter waited until the men had gone ahead and then followed, keeping to the shadows so he could not be seen.

The guards marched Jesus away to the house of Caiaphas, the high priest. The religious leaders had gathered to put Jesus on trial.

'Tell us whether you are the Christ, the Son of God,' they demanded.

Jesus simply said, 'You have said it yourself.'

Caiaphas was very angry! How could this man claim to be God?

'This is blasphemy!' he said. 'This is a crime worthy of death – and we have the evidence we need to condemn you!'

The men spat at Jesus and hit him. All this time, Peter was waiting outside in the shadows.

Help us not to run away when things are difficult but to stand up for what we think is right.

Have you ever let someone down badly?

Peter loved Jesus with all his heart. But when he was afraid, he did the wrong thing.

 Matthew 26:69-75

While Peter was waiting in the courtyard of the high priest's house, he became aware that a servant girl was staring at him.

'Aren't you a friend of that man in there?' she asked him.

'No!' said Peter. 'I don't know what you mean.'

Then another girl came and accused him too. 'Yes, he was with Jesus!' she said.

'No – you're wrong! I don't know the man,' Peter said.

Then someone else said he had the same accent as Jesus. Peter was afraid of what they would do to him. He denied it a third time.

Then he heard the cockerel crow… It was morning. Peter remembered that Jesus had said that he would deny him three times before morning.
Peter cried with shame.

Help us to love you in the good times and in the bad times, Lord.

306

When good men do nothing…

Sometimes we must act to stop bad things happening.

📖 *Matthew 27:1-2, 11-26*

Pontius Pilate was the Roman governor in charge of the area. Only he could decide if someone should die. The religious leaders took Jesus to him in chains.

'This man is a troublemaker,' the chief priests told Pilate.

Pilate questioned Jesus. He could tell he was innocent of any crime but he didn't want more trouble. Outside, a bloodthirsty crowd, bribed by the religious leaders, was shouting.

'Crucify him! Crucify him!' they said.

Pontius Pilate was afraid.

'I can set a prisoner free as it is Passover,' he said. 'Barabbas, the murderer? Or the man you call your King – Jesus from Nazareth? Who do you want?'

'Free Barabbas!' they shouted.

'Then what about Jesus?' Pilate asked.

'Crucify him!' they shouted.

Pilate washed his hands in a bowl of water.

'This is not my fault,' he said. 'This is what you wanted.' Then he handed Jesus over to be crucified.

Lord, help us to be active in doing good; and active in standing up for others when they need our help.

Jesus' suffering

Jesus was betrayed and humiliated; he suffered pain till his body could take it no longer and then he died.

 Matthew 27:27-37

It was a Friday morning when the Roman soldiers took Jesus away. They dressed him in a scarlet robe and put a stick in his hand.

'You're supposed to be a king, aren't you?' they said, laughing. 'You need a crown!'

The soldiers beat him and pushed a crown of sharp thorns on to his head.

As they were on the way to the place of execution they came across a man called Simon who came from Cyrene, in Africa, and forced him to carry Jesus' cross.

Then they went out to an area known as Golgotha, and nailed him to a cross between two thieves. The soldiers threw dice to divide up his clothes among themselves and watched him as he suffered there.

Above him was a sign that said, 'This is Jesus, the King of the Jews.'

Thank you, Lord, for all you did for me, for us. Thank you that even if I were the only person who sinned, you would still have gone to the cross for me.

Can anyone be forgiven?

It was not too late even for the thief dying on the cross.

 Luke 23:35-43

The religious leaders watched as Jesus hung on the cross and laughed together.

'If Jesus is really God's Chosen One, let's see if he can save himself – he was always so good at helping others!'

One of the thieves hanging on a cross beside him also raised his head and spoke to him.

'You saved other people: why don't you save yourself – and us too!'

But the other thief said, 'Leave him alone! Are you not afraid of God even as you are dying? We deserve our punishment but he does not.' Then he said to Jesus, 'Please, remember me.'

Jesus answered, 'Today, I promise you, you will be with me in heaven.'

Thank you, Lord, that you will forgive anyone who comes to you.

Thinking of others

Jesus was selfless: even in his pain and suffering he was thinking about the needs of other people.

 John 19:26-27

Long hours passed while Jesus was suffering on the cross.

Some people nearby were weeping for him.

One of his disciples was nearby comforting his mother. 'Mother!' Jesus breathed. 'Here is John – treat him as your son now.'

Then he looked at John. 'Look after Mary. Take care of her as if she were your own mother.'

John was very sad to see Jesus suffering. Together he and Mary stood waiting, knowing that soon Jesus would die.

Help us to follow your example, Lord, and always think of others before we think of our own needs.

The humility of Jesus

The apostle Paul told the church in Philippi to follow the example of Jesus.

📖 Philippians 2:3-11

310

Teach us not to be selfish, Lord. Help us to be the people you want us to be.

'Try not to be selfish. When you stop thinking about yourself you will stop trying to make a good impression on others but instead be the person God wants you to be.

'Be humble and think of others as better than yourself. Don't be so caught up in things that matter to you that you have no time for those around you. Take an interest in what others are doing, listen to them.

'Be like Jesus, who was God himself, yet did not behave as though he were above all of us. He was born in human form to an unmarried mother and humbled himself even further when he died the painful and humiliating death of a criminal on a cross.

'It is for this reason that God gave him a name that is above every other name, so that at the name of Jesus every knee shall bow and everyone will one day know that he is Lord of all.'

Are we only Christians on Sundays?

The apostle Paul encouraged the church in Philippi to live godly lives all the time.

📖 *Philippians 2:12-16*

'When I was there with you, you were careful to be guided by me. I need you to keep doing good things and act as if you belong to Jesus even when I am not there.

'Obey God – love him and respect him and avoid all those things which you know displease him. God is at work within you, helping you to want to obey him, and then helping you do the things he wants.

'Try not to complain, don't argue; then no one can point the finger at you and say you are letting God down. Even when things around you are wrong or corrupt and unhelpful, be different. Stand out as Christian people who are like Christ and whose lives are without blame.'

Lord, help me to be a Christian all the week long and not just when other Christian people can see what I am doing.

312

Thank you that our sins are forgiven because of what you did, Lord – and it does not depend on our goodness.

Knowing Jesus

What is the most important thing in your life? Paul is clear that for him it is Jesus.

 Philippians 3:4-9

'I was born into a religious family and kept the rules and thought that was what God wanted.

'But then I met Jesus. I realized that all the things I thought were valuable were really worthless. The only thing that matters, the only thing worth living for, is to know Jesus.

'God has made us his friends not because of what we have done but because of what Jesus has done. I want to know Jesus, and I want to know the power of God that raised him from death to life, the same resurrection that one day I will also know.

'I have left everything else behind so that nothing gets in the way of my relationship with him. I don't need to be good enough; I cannot save myself by keeping rules. I trust Jesus to save me; faith in his death on the cross for me is enough.'

Who do we want to be?

Paul wanted to be the person who deserved the sacrifice Jesus made for him.

 Philippians 3:10-14

'The only way for me to really know Jesus is to put aside everything else so I can experience the power that brought him back to life again.

'Whatever it takes, I want to live my life as a new person, living for Jesus, living as Jesus did and putting him first in my life.

'I am not perfect – of course I am not! There is still so much I have to learn. But I am working towards the day when I will finally be everything that God wants me to be, the person who deserves the death that Jesus died for.

'Now I am ready to forget all that is past and look forward to what lies ahead, like a runner who is straining to reach the end of the race and bursts through the finishing tape to receive the prize which God has ready for everyone who trusts in Jesus' death and resurrection.'

Lord, help us, like Paul, to run the Christian race and never give up.

Why did Jesus die?

Jesus did not die because of anything he had done wrong, but in the place of all the people in the world who had ever done bad things.

 Matthew 27:45-55

Jesus hung on the cross for most of that sad Friday. From midday the sky turned black and people stood in darkness. Jesus felt very much alone.

It was about 3.00pm that they heard Jesus cry out, 'My God, my God, why have you deserted me?'

Someone tried to offer something to moisten his lips but Jesus cried out again and then breathed his last breath.

At that moment the earth shook, and people all around were terrified. 'This man was surely the Son of God!' said one.

Among those who stood watching Jesus die were Mary Magdalene and the mother of two of his close friends, James and John.

Lord, thank you that you suffered and died in my place on that cross, for all the bad things I have done.

Taking risks for Jesus

Are you afraid to be known as Jesus' friend?

 Mark 15:42-46, John 19:38-42

It was Friday, and drawing towards the Sabbath day.

A rich man from Arimathea called Joseph had been one of Jesus' friends. He went bravely to Pilate and asked if he could take down Jesus' body from the cross before the Sabbath began.

Pilate was suspicious. Was Jesus really dead? Was he dead already? He called for the soldier who had been there with Jesus on the cross. He confirmed that he had checked carefully that Jesus was indeed dead.

Then Pilate allowed Joseph to take down the body from the cross. Joseph and Nicodemus wrapped Jesus' body in a long sheet of linen and placed it in a burial tomb in a garden nearby. Then they rolled a stone in front of the entrance.

Lord, I love you. Help me not to be afraid to tell others that I am your friend.

316

Do you share what you learn with others?

Mary shared with Peter and John – but did John tell the others what he had realized?

 John 20:1-10

The day after Jesus was buried was the Sabbath, a special day of rest. So it was early on Sunday morning, while it was still dark, that Mary Magdalene went to visit the place where she had seen Jesus buried. Her sadness turned to shock to find the stone had been rolled away from the entrance – and the tomb was empty.

Mary ran to find Peter and John and they went to see for themselves. They saw the empty tomb, and that the linen coverings that had wrapped his body were still there.

Then John finally understood what Jesus had meant when he had told them that he would rise from the dead: Jesus had died – but now he was alive!

Lord, as we learn more about you, day by day, help us to help each other with what we learn.

Seeing is believing...

Faith is trusting God and others for what we cannot see for ourselves.

 John 20:11-18

Mary still did not understand where Jesus was. She stayed weeping in the garden when the men went home.

Then two angels asked Mary why she was crying and tried to comfort her.

'Someone has taken Jesus away!' she wept. 'And I don't know where they have put him.'

Then Mary realized someone else was there but she couldn't see him through her tears. Then he spoke her name: 'Mary...'

Mary knew that voice. It was Jesus! Then she also realized that he was not dead any more. Jesus was alive and he was here talking to her! Mary was so excited she could not wait to tell his other friends!

Thank you, Lord, for all who have shared the good news of your life, death and resurrection with me.

318

Jesus changes everything

Having Jesus in our lives means we don't need to be afraid, or lonely, or sad any more.

John 20:19-23

Thank you for being in our lives, Lord, so we don't need to be sad, or afraid or lonely.

It was Sunday evening. Some of the disciples were hiding together in a room with the doors locked because they were afraid that soldiers might arrest them too.

Suddenly, everything changed. They were no longer alone. Jesus was there in the room with them!

'You're alive!' they shouted. They were so pleased to see him. But how had he entered the room?

Then Jesus showed them the marks where the nails had hurt him. Now they understood that he had died – but he had risen from the dead. It was another miracle.

Meeting Jesus…

Was recognizing who Jesus was a sudden event for you – or did it take place gradually?

Luke 24:13-35

Two of the disciples were travelling to Emmaus on that same Sunday, talking to each other about Jesus' arrest and crucifixion – and now his resurrection from the dead.

    While they were walking, someone joined them and they told him about everything they had been discussing.

    Then the stranger began to tell them how the scriptures said that one day all these things would take place – and it had all happened in their lifetime to someone they knew.

    When they arrived at Emmaus, they invited the man to eat with them. As soon as he broke the bread and asked God to bless it – they realized that this was no stranger at all – it was Jesus!

Thank you, Lord, that you make sense of everything for us.

Do you enjoy being with other believers?

Sometimes we miss out by not being where other Christians are.

 John 20:24-28

Thomas had not been with the other disciples when Jesus had come into the locked room. Now he did not believe them when they said that Jesus was alive.

'I must see him with my own eyes,' he said, 'and put my fingers in his wounds to be quite sure.'

Eight days later, Jesus appeared again in the same way even though the doors were locked.

'Look at the nail marks, Thomas,' Jesus said. 'Put your hands here in the wound at my side. Do you believe it's me, now?'

Thomas fell to his knees. It really was Jesus!

'My Lord and my God!' he said.

I am sorry, Lord, when I find it hard to trust you.

Does Jesus make a difference in your life?

When we are feeling down or nothing seems to be going right, spending time with Jesus can change everything.

📖 *John 21:1-12*

'Let's go fishing,' Peter said to his friends one evening.

Seven of the disciples went out that night but after many hours on Lake Galilee, they hadn't caught anything. It was nearly dawn when a man called to them from the shore.

'Throw your net on the right side of the boat!'

When Peter did, the net was filled with 153 fish! The man on the shore was Jesus! Peter jumped into the water and left his friends to bring in the catch of fish while he swam to shore.

There was a fire and warm bread waiting for them.

'Bring some of those fish,' Jesus said. 'Let's have breakfast together.'

Thank you, Lord, that you are always there when we most need you.

Jesus understands us

Even when we feel guilty or ashamed and don't even like ourselves – we can tell Jesus all about it.

📖 *John 21:15-17*

Peter had not had a chance to talk to Jesus alone since that terrible night when he told people that Jesus was not his friend.

Jesus knew that Peter felt guilty and wanted to tell him how awful he felt.

Jesus asked Peter the same question three times, just as Peter had denied him three times.

'Peter, do you love me more than the others do?' he asked.

'Yes, I do, Lord! You know I do!'

Then Jesus gave to Peter a huge task. 'Peter, I have a special job for you to do,' Jesus said. 'I want you to look after my followers.'

Your forgiveness sets us free! Thank you, Lord!

Do you like to wait?

Jesus had ascended into heaven and the Holy Spirit had yet to come – how do you think the disciples felt?

 Acts 1:1-11

More than a month had passed since Jesus had risen from the dead. He had spent more time with his friends and it had been very special. But now Jesus was ready to return to his Father in heaven.

'I must go very soon,' he told his friends. 'But don't be afraid. I will not leave you alone. Wait in Jerusalem and the Holy Spirit will come to you. It will be as if I were always there to help you, wherever you are, whenever you need me.'

Then suddenly Jesus was gone. Two angels appeared.

'Don't look for Jesus on earth any more,' they said. 'He is in heaven. But one day he will come back.'

Help me, Lord, to wait patiently for your promises to come true.

324

Am I good enough to go to heaven?

God accepts us not because of what we have done but because of what Jesus has done.

📖 Romans 3:21-24

'God has shown us that the only way to heaven doesn't rely on us being perfect or trying to do good things all the time (and often failing),' said the apostle Paul. 'We don't have to be "good enough". Instead God will accept us just as we are if we trust Jesus to take away our sins.

'It doesn't matter who we are or what we have done. Every one of us has sinned; none of us is perfect; but God accepts us because Jesus is perfect – and has taken the punishment for all we have done wrong.'

Thank you, thank you, Lord Jesus, for taking my punishment on the cross.

What it means to be a Christian

Can others see the difference that Jesus makes in your life?

 Colossians 3:1-10

'Are you looking forward to heaven and all the good things it offers us?' asked Paul. 'Can you imagine how happy we will be to know God's love face to face, where there is no unkindness or pain or fear? Think about that – and don't worry so much about the things that seem like big problems now.

'There should be no place in your life for worshipping yourself and all that you want; or for bad temper or bad language, or bad feelings towards others or gossiping about them.'

Forgive me, Lord, when I am angry and say horrible things to other people…

The power to do good

326

The Holy Spirit comes to all believers and helps us to be the hands and feet and voice of Jesus in the world.

Lord, use my hands and feet and voice today to be some good in my part of the world.

📖 *Acts 1, 2:1-4*

All Jesus' friends gathered in Jerusalem for the harvest festival known as Pentecost, around 120 of them. Many others had come from all over the world to celebrate. The city was buzzing with people speaking different languages.

Jesus' friends were together in a house in Jerusalem for the celebrations when suddenly the Holy Spirit came to them. They heard a sound like a rushing wind and saw what looked like tongues of fire on each person. They realized that the Holy Spirit had given them strength to do the good things that Jesus wanted them to do. It was as if Jesus were there with them all the time wherever they went. They would never feel alone.

Peter, a changed person

Can people see changes in you because you love Jesus?

📖 Acts 2:14-36

Peter had been afraid once to tell people that Jesus was his friend. But now he was not only able to stand up and speak to a huge crowd, he could speak in languages he had never learned. They all could!

The house had been filled with sound on the day of Pentecost, and now a crowd had gathered outside. Peter went out to talk to them.

'Do you remember Jesus?' he asked. 'You crucified him! But God gave him new life – and we saw him and talked with him ourselves! We are witnesses of his resurrection!

'Now he will forgive anyone who believes Jesus is God's Son. Come now and tell him that you are sorry and you can be his friend too.'

About 3,000 people became Christians that day.

Lord, thank you, that every new person who comes to you for forgiveness causes great joy in heaven.

One big family

What are the good things about being a family? What are the problems?

 Galatians 3:11, 26-29

'We are all God's friends because we have faith in Jesus and believe he died on the cross for us.

'This also makes us God's children – so together we are one big family. We are no longer people from different countries or backgrounds or people who went to different schools; we are no longer black or white or any colour in between; we are not even men or women, boys or girls; but we are all the same: we are Christians, united because of our faith in Jesus. All the promises God made long ago to Abraham now apply to us too, along with all the blessings God gave him.'

Thank you, Lord, that we are all equal as Christians, brothers and sisters together.

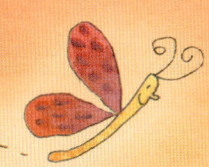

Have you ever said something you shouldn't have?

Friendships and trust can be completely destroyed by the things we say.

📖 *James 3:1-12, 17-18*

'Try not to tell others their faults – after all, we all make mistakes,' said James.

'One of the most important things you can learn is how to control what you say. Your tongue is such a small thing, but it can do great harm to others. The same tongue that praises God and thanks him for all his blessings can say cruel things to others or say bad things about them behind their backs. People may never forget those cruel words.

'Try not to make trouble but give way to others or discuss things in a friendly way. Only good things come from being a peacemaker.'

Please help me to be a peacemaker, Lord, not a troublemaker.

330

More than we ask for…

Sometimes God answers our prayers in unexpected ways.

 Acts 3:1-10

Thank you that you are generous, Lord, and your love knows no limits.

A man who could not walk sat by one of the temple gates begging day after day. Peter and John saw him there as they went to the temple to pray.

'Do you have any money?' the man asked them. 'Can you spare any coins?'

Peter smiled at the man. 'I don't have any money I can share with you,' Peter said, 'but with Jesus' help, I can offer you a much greater gift. I can help you to walk.'

Then by the power of the Holy Spirit, the man was healed! He got to his feet and thanked God for healing him. Then he jumped up and down with joy as people turned to stare in amazement.

Unexpected results

Doing the right thing doesn't always make us popular…

📖 *Acts 4:1-4*

Everyone who went to the temple knew the man who had been healed. They had seen him begging there every day. So now they saw that a miracle had happened. A man who could not walk was walking. But how? Everyone was amazed.

'Why are you surprised?' Peter asked them. 'You allowed Pilate to crucify Jesus. You saw that he died and was buried. But God raised him to new life. That was a miracle and so is this. A paralyzed man can walk because of the power of the Holy Spirit.'

The temple guards didn't like this at all. They grabbed Peter and John and threw them into prison.

331

Help me to say and do the right thing, Lord, even if it means people won't like me.

Is good news not worth sharing?

Whatever happened, the disciples could not keep what they had learned about Jesus to themselves!

📖 Acts 4:5-18

After a night in prison, Peter and John were questioned the next morning.

'How did you heal this man?'

The Holy Spirit helped Peter to answer, just as Jesus had promised.

'We didn't – Jesus healed him. And only Jesus can heal and forgive and save any of us.'

The religious leaders knew they could not keep Peter and John in prison because many people had already seen the miracle for themselves – they knew it was true.

'OK, we will let you go – but only if you promise not to keep talking about Jesus and his teaching.'

'We cannot help tell everyone about Jesus!' they said. 'Who do you think we should obey – you or God himself?'

Help me to share the good things you have done for me, Lord – because I can't help it!

Living the way Jesus taught

How easy is it for us to give up what we own to help others?

📖 Acts 4:4, 21-36

There were now about 5,000 believers in Jerusalem, brought together with one belief and one purpose.

They felt that all the things they owned did not belong to them any more, but were gifts from God, so they shared everything with each other, living the way that Jesus had taught them. They sold their houses or fields so that the money could be used to help those in need.

'Help us not to be afraid as we tell people about you, Lord,' they prayed. 'Let people see the miracles done in your name and know that you are the true and living God so that they can know you for themselves.'

Lord, I want to value people more than things – please help me when I find it hard.

The truth hurts

Do we get angry when people tell us what we have done wrong?

📖 Acts 6:1 – 7:60

The disciples chose seven men to help them look after people who were ill or poor. Stephen was one of them.

God blessed Stephen with many gifts: he was able to heal people and speak bravely about Jesus. Many people became Christians because they saw that, like Jesus, Stephen was kind and loving.

But the religious leaders hated him. When he told them that they had betrayed and murdered the person God had sent to save them, they dragged him out of the city and began to stone him to death.

'Lord, forgive them for what they are doing!' said Stephen, just before he died.

Lord, please take care of people in parts of the world where they cannot worship you freely or safely.

When people are sure they are right…

How do we treat people who disagree with us?

 Acts 8:1-3

Saul believed in God. He was a very religious man but he was sure that the Christians were wrong about Jesus and hated all that they said and did. So when Stephen was killed, Saul looked on, pleased at what had happened.

Then he and others began to make trouble for all the new believers. Saul himself went from house to house, looking for people like Stephen and throwing them into prison. He would not rest until they were all stopped from telling people about Jesus.

Help me, Lord, to listen to and respect the views of others, even if they are not the same as mine.

336

Do we use every opportunity God gives us?

Wherever we are and whoever we meet, we can share God's love with others.

 Acts 8:4-8

The new Christians had asked for God's help. Now they needed it more than ever. Those who were not caught and put in prison left Jerusalem quickly to hide from Saul; but wherever they went, they told people about Jesus.

    Philip went to Samaria and healed people who were disabled and told them how to love God and follow Jesus. There were many very happy people in Samaria while Philip was there.

Lord, you are great! Even when people try to hurt us, you make other good things happen!

God needs us!

How can people come to trust Jesus if we do not share what we know?

 *Acts 8:26-38*

Philip was praying, listening to what God wanted him to do. God told him to go down to the road between Jerusalem and Gaza. Philip did not know why but when he got there he met an important man from Ethiopia reading aloud from one of the prophecies about Jesus. The Holy Spirit told Philip to go to the man.

'Do you understand what you are reading?' Philip asked him.

'No, I need some help,' the man replied.

So Philip told him that God had sent Jesus, his Son, to die on a cross in the place of anyone who had ever done something wrong.

'Look, here is some water!' said the man. 'I believe that Jesus died for me too – please baptize me!'

Lord, make me ready to listen and to act, to tell people around me that you love them.

338

What things do we do that hurt Jesus?

When we are not kind to others, or don't do something good when we could, we let Jesus down.

 Acts 9:3-8

Saul was still trying to find the followers of Jesus to put them in prison. He was travelling with friends to Damascus to bring back in chains any he could find.

'Saul, why are you persecuting me?' came a voice.

Saul could not see where the voice came from.

'Who are you?' asked Saul.

'I am Jesus, and you are hurting me with all these bad things you are doing,' came the answer. 'Listen to me. I have an important job for you to do.'

Saul's friends also heard the voice but saw no one. They had to lead Saul by the hand to Damascus because now he could not see.

I am so sorry, Lord, because I know I have let you down. Forgive me because…

The way prayer works

God guides us to be the answer to the prayers of someone else if we take time to listen to him.

339

📖 Acts 9:10-15

In Damascus God spoke in a vision to a man named Ananias.

'Ananias!' God said. 'I want you to go to Straight Street, to the house of Judas. Ask for a man from Tarsus named Saul. He is praying to me now and needs your help. Go and lay your hands on him so that he can see again. I have told him you are coming.'

'But Lord,' said Ananias, 'this man has done terrible things to the believers in Jerusalem! He has come to arrest us all!'

'Trust me, Ananias. Go and do this for me because I have chosen Saul to take my message to people outside the Jewish nation so everyone can know that I love them.'

Open my ears to hear you, Lord, and to do what you ask.

When trusting God is hard…

Sometimes we need to let go of what seems to make sense and do what God tells us.

 Acts 9:17-20

Ananias did what God asked him to do. He went and found Saul and laid his hands on him so that he would be healed.

'Brother Saul, the Lord Jesus, who spoke to you as you were travelling here, has sent me. He wants you to see again and be filled with the Holy Spirit.'

At that moment Saul's eyes cleared; he was no longer blind. Then he got up and was baptized. He had something to eat and began to recover from all that had happened while staying in Damascus for a few days.

Lord, you know everything. Help me to trust you, when doing the right thing is difficult.

What happens when we meet Jesus?

Faith turns our lives around and brings real change.

📖 *Acts 9:20-27*

Saul went to the synagogues in Damascus and started to tell everyone there that Jesus really was God's Son.

At first, no one could believe the change in him. 'Surely this man is our enemy?' they said. 'Hasn't he come here to arrest those who follow Jesus?'

Then people began to listen and believed what he told them. But some of the Jews were angry. They waited at the city gate to try to catch him and kill him.

Saul was warned of their plot. During the night some of the believers secretly lowered him through an opening in the city wall.

When Saul arrived in Jerusalem, he had trouble making other believers trust him until Barnabas told them about what had happened.

Lord, I want others to see that my life is different because I love you.

342

Taking things to God in prayer

Do we spend more time talking about a problem than praying about it?

 Acts 9:36-42

Peter travelled from place to place, healing and helping people. In Joppa he was asked to come to the bedside of a woman who had just died.

There were many unhappy people there all busy telling him how kind Tabitha was and how she was always helping anyone in need. The room was full of people. Peter sent everyone away so he could pray for her.

Then he said to the woman, 'Get up, Tabitha.' And the woman opened her eyes and sat up.

When all her friends came into the room, they were amazed! As people heard about it, they too became believers.

After this Peter went to the home of a tanner called Simon and stayed in Joppa for a while.

Help us, Lord, to share all our worries and all our problems with you.

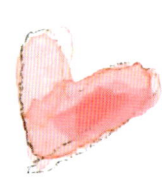

Faith leads to kind actions

God loves to see us putting what we believe into practice.

📖 *Acts 10:1-8*

Cornelius was a Roman soldier from the Italian Regiment. While working in Israel, Cornelius and his family had come to love God and they gave generously to people in need. They often prayed together.

So when an angel appeared one day with a message for him, Cornelius listened.

'God has heard your prayers, Cornelius, and seen the good things you do,' said the angel. 'Now, go to find Peter who is in a house by the sea in Joppa. He has so much more he can teach you.'

Lord, teach me so that I get to know you better every day.

The power of praying people

When we pray, God helps not just us but others too.

📖 Acts 10:9-16

Peter was praying on the roof of Simon's house in Joppa.

Peter was hungry and while he prayed, he had a vision. He saw that God was offering him all kinds of birds and animals to eat, including those normally forbidden to Jewish men and women.

'But these animals aren't clean, Lord,' Peter said. 'I mustn't eat them.'

God replied, 'Once that was true, but now I have made them clean and holy.'

The same thing happened three times before all the animals disappeared again. While Peter was wondering what the vision could mean, he heard someone call to him from the gate of the house.

The Holy Spirit told Peter to go with the men at the gate to Cornelius' house.

Lord, make us willing to be the answer to someone else's prayers.

Does God have favourites?

All are welcome in God's family, no matter where they come from or what they have done.

 Acts 10:24-48

The next day Peter went with the men to the soldier's house in Caesarea where Cornelius had gathered his family and friends. Peter and his friends had always believed that they were God's holy chosen people and God's offer of new life was for them alone. Now Peter understood his strange vision. God was telling him that Jesus had come to make everyone welcome in God's kingdom – even Roman soldiers and their families.

'God has no favourites,' Peter told the people gathered in the house. 'Everyone who believes that Jesus died for their sins will be forgiven. God loves you and welcomes you into his kingdom too.'

Then the Holy Spirit came to Cornelius and all the people there and they were baptized as Christians.

Thank you, Lord, that you accept all who come to you – even me...

Do you value your freedom to worship God?

Many people in the world still have to worship in secret.

📖 *Acts 12:1-5*

Herod Agrippa was now the Roman king in Judea. He began to treat the Christians badly and had James, John's brother, put to death with a sword. Then he put Peter in prison, planning to give him a public trial before killing him too.

So Peter spent Passover in chains in a dark cell with a guard on either side of him and two more soldiers guarding the door. He was very sad about what had happened to James; he also knew that Herod would probably put him to death the next day or soon afterwards.

While he was in prison, many of the believers gathered in the house of John Mark's mother and prayed for Peter.

Lord, we pray for all those who do not have freedom to worship together or speak openly about your love.

Are we ready for the answers God gives us?

God speaks in many ways and sometimes great miracles happen.

 Acts 12:6-11

God answered their prayers by sending an angel to set Peter free!

'Quickly! Get up!' said the angel. As Peter stood up, the chains fell from his wrists, freeing him from the guards sleeping beside him.

Peter followed the angel past the guards and then the locked gates of the prison swung open in front of them… Peter went to John Mark's house and banged on the door.

Rhoda went to the door but was so excited to hear Peter's voice, she ran to tell the others without opening it.

'It can't be Peter!' they said – but the knocking went on until they let Peter in! He quickly explained what had happened: God had answered their prayers with a miracle.

Lord, make us ready. Help us to pray expecting great things to happen.

Can you praise God even when things go badly?

Paul seemed to walk into trouble wherever he went while trying to do what God wanted. But he still trusted God.

📖 Acts 16:16-25

When Paul and his friend Silas were in Philippi, they met a slave girl who made her masters rich by predicting the future. The girl knew that Paul was a Christian and that he was there to show people how to find God.

Paul set the girl free of the evil spirit inside her – but as a result she could no longer see the future. Her masters were so angry, Paul and Silas were beaten and thrown into prison with their feet in the stocks, carefully guarded by a jailor.

That night Paul and Silas sang hymns to God. They praised God just the same.

Please help me to do what is right, even when it makes me unpopular.

Have you ever told a stranger about your faith?

Paul didn't force his faith on the prison jailor, he simply answered his question.

 Acts 16:26-34

The rumble of an earthquake stopped the singing in the prison cell. The ground moved beneath the prison and the doors flew open. Paul and Silas found their chains no longer bound them.

The jailer was terrified. He thought his prisoners would surely have escaped in the darkness and drew his sword to kill himself.

'Stop!' Paul shouted. 'We are all still here.'

'But how can I be saved?' said the jailor.

'Trust Jesus and you will be saved,' Paul answered.

While the jailor washed their wounds, Paul and Silas told him and all his family about Jesus. They all became Christians and were baptized that night.

Help me always to be ready to answer questions about my faith so that others might know the joy of knowing you too.

Would you give up if people laughed at you for your faith?

Paul suffered greatly because he loved Jesus. But he knew what Jesus had suffered for him. He would not give up.

📖 Acts 21:15 – 26:32

Paul had left his home behind long ago. Now nothing was more important than sharing his faith with others.

Paul was not always welcome. Sometimes people threw stones at him and drove him away. He was whipped or beaten and starved. But as long as he could walk and speak, Paul would spread the good news about Jesus.

After years of suffering along the way, Paul went back to Jerusalem – where he was arrested and imprisoned. Some time passed before he asked to see the emperor in Rome because he was a Roman citizen.

Help me to be brave as Paul was, Lord. Help me to stand up for my faith.

How easy is it for you to trust God?

Have you ever been in a situation where everything seems to be going wrong? Paul knew that God could always be trusted.

 Acts 27:1-25

Paul had a friend called Luke who was a doctor. When Paul was sent to Rome by ship, he was placed in the care of a soldier called Julius and Luke was allowed to travel with him.

The journey was not an easy one. At first strong winds delayed them but after some time they sailed through a violent storm and the sky went completely dark. The ship lurched up and down and waves crashed on to the deck. All on board were afraid for their lives!

But God spoke to Paul and told him that none of them would die. Paul trusted God.

Help us, Lord, to turn to you and to trust you when we are afraid.

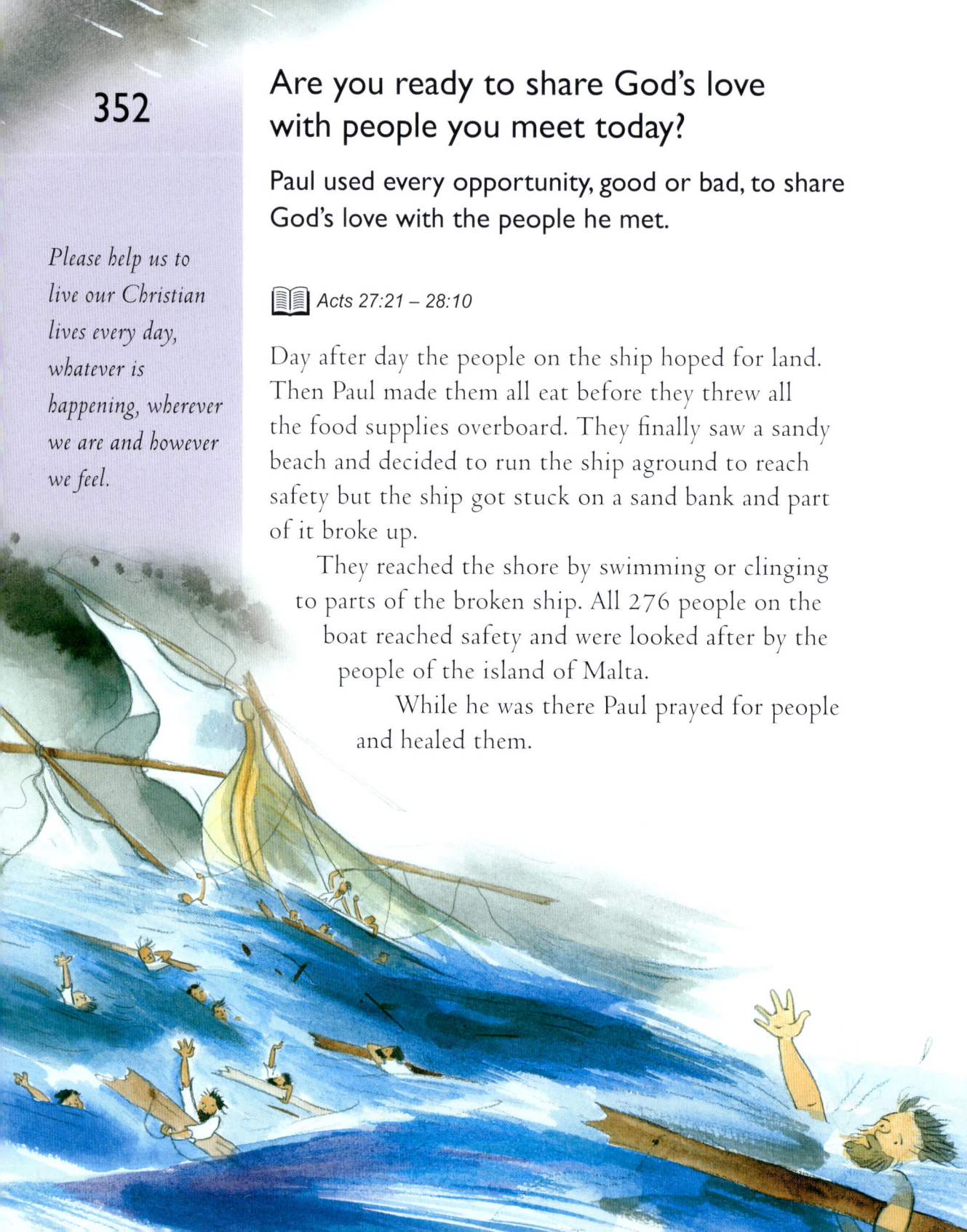

352

Please help us to live our Christian lives every day, whatever is happening, wherever we are and however we feel.

Are you ready to share God's love with people you meet today?

Paul used every opportunity, good or bad, to share God's love with the people he met.

📖 Acts 27:21 – 28:10

Day after day the people on the ship hoped for land. Then Paul made them all eat before they threw all the food supplies overboard. They finally saw a sandy beach and decided to run the ship aground to reach safety but the ship got stuck on a sand bank and part of it broke up.

They reached the shore by swimming or clinging to parts of the broken ship. All 276 people on the boat reached safety and were looked after by the people of the island of Malta.

While he was there Paul prayed for people and healed them.

What matters more to you than anything else?

For Paul, it was his Christian faith.

 Acts 28:11-30

Paul finally set sail again for Rome three months after the shipwreck but when he arrived there, no one was expecting him. Instead of a trial, he was allowed to live wherever he liked, as long as there was a soldier there to guard him.

For two years Paul welcomed people from Rome to visit him.

'God loves you,' he told them. 'Jesus died for you on the cross so that you can know God's forgiveness and the help of the Holy Spirit in your lives.'

Some believed him, became Christians and were baptized; others did not.

Paul used his time in Rome to write many letters to the churches he had visited on his travels, offering them help and advice.

Thank you, Lord, for those who shared their faith with me, for my family, teachers and church leaders.

354

Lord, please take all of us, heart, mind and soul – to serve you today.

How can we show God we love him?

The apostle Paul told the Christians in Rome how to give their lives to God.

 Romans 12:1-2

'Do you think often about what God has done for you? Do you wonder how you can ever show him how grateful you are?

'I will tell you what to do. I will tell you what God wants most of all. God wants all of you – heart, mind and soul. He wants you to give yourself to him, not as a dead sacrifice but living for him each day, trying to do what is right and good.

'Don't copy the behaviour of people who don't love God. Be different. Stand out from the crowd by the way you think and the things you do. And you will find real joy, deep down, in living this way.'

All working together

The apostle Paul told the Christians in Corinth that God brings us together into one 'body'.

📖 *1 Corinthians 12:12-20*

'You and I each have one body, but it has many different parts all working together. It is the same with the body of Christ.

'When we were baptized by the Holy Spirit we all, though different, came together to form one body. It doesn't matter where we came from or what our background is, God treats us the same way.

'If a foot should say, 'I don't belong to the body because I am not a hand', it would still belong to the body. If an ear should say, 'I don't belong to the body because I am not an eye,' it would still belong to the body.

'We are all different but God has brought us together and joined us together.'

Help us, Lord, to accept each other just as you accept us so we can be useful together.

356

Lord, help us to weep with those who are sad and be happy with those who have good news.

We need each other

As parts of the body of Christ, we should care for and value each other.

 1 Corinthians 12:21-26

'If the whole body were an eye, how would we hear? If the whole body were an ear, how would we smell? The eye needs the hand, and the head needs the feet. We need the parts of the body that seem weaker or less beautiful – all the parts of the body do what they need to do; all are important.

'So when God brings us together into one body or church he wants us to be united, joined together with one purpose, caring for each other and valuing each other.

'If one suffers, the rest share that suffering too; if good things happen to another, the rest share that joy with them.'

What is the most important gift?

All gifts are valuable but the best of all gifts is love…

📖 1 Corinthians 12:27 – 13:3

'All Christians are part of the body of Christ and God has given gifts to all.

'Is everyone an apostle? No. Is everyone a prophet or teacher? No. Does everyone have the gift of healing or helping or guiding, speaking in other languages or interpreting them? No.

'It is good to pray that God will bless you with gifts for the good of everyone – but desire most of all that God will help you to love.

'Speaking in other languages without learning them; knowing what will happen in the future; having faith to move mountains – even giving all I have to the poor: if I didn't love others, it would be of no value at all.'

Help us, Lord, to use our gifts for the good of others, not to boast; and to value the gift of love above all others.

What does real love look like?

How different life would be if we all showed this kind of love in our lives.

 1 Corinthians 13:4-7

'Love is patient and kind; it is never jealous or envious, never boastful or proud, never haughty or selfish or rude.' said Paul.

'Love does not demand to have its own way. It is not over sensitive or bad tempered. Love does not hold grudges against others and hardly notices when others get things wrong.

'Love is never glad when people are treated unfairly but it is always happy when lies fall away and the truth shines out.

'If you love someone, you will be loyal no matter what it costs. You will always believe in them, always expect the best of them, and always defend them against others.'

Please forgive us when our love doesn't match up to your love. May our love be more like your love, day by day.

Can people see Jesus in us?

The apostle Paul reminded the Christians in Corinth that their lives should show that they love Jesus.

📖 2 Corinthians 5:14-17

'Since we believe that Jesus died for us on the cross we know that we have changed from being our old selves to being someone new. The selfish person we once were has died…

'Jesus died so that we could live for ever – and now we live not just to please ourselves but to live each day as Jesus wants us to.

'When someone becomes a Christian, he becomes a brand new person inside. That person is not the same anymore. A new life has begun!'

We don't want to be selfish people, Lord. Let that new person be the one people see in us today.

What does God want?

God is the creator of all that is good and fair and he hates it when we treat others badly.

📖 Amos 5:6-15, 21-24

'Seek God, your maker!' said the prophet Amos. 'God has seen the things you do and so many of them are wrong. You hate people who are honest and you steal from the poor. You use your power to treat people badly and unfairly.

'Stop acting this way!' said Amos. 'Do what is right and good instead so that God will be on your side. Hate all that is bad, love what is good; turn yourselves around and act fairly.

'The Lord is not interested in the gifts you bring to him and won't listen to the hymns of praise you sing! What he wants from you is justice – justice rolling down like rivers and a stream flowing full of all that is good.'

Lord, help me to treat others as I would want to be treated myself.

How can we show that God is in our lives?

Peter, like Paul and Jesus himself, urged us to be practical in showing love to others.

 *1 Peter 4:8-11*

'Show real love for each other – it makes up for so many other things,' said Peter, the friend of Jesus. 'Be quick to offer to share your home with those who need a meal or a place to stay.

'God has given us all gifts to use for the good of everyone. If you are good at speaking, make sure what you say helps others to know what God is saying. If you have the gift of helping others, do it as often as you can with all the energy that God himself gives you.

'In this way people will see that God is working through you and thank him for it.'

I want to show my love in the things that I do, Lord. Show me how today.

362

How does God treat us like his children?

God shows us where we go wrong and corrects us.

📖 Hebrews 12:5-13

God is our father. He loves us and treats us as his children. But that doesn't mean he wants us to do bad things whenever we want to!

Sometimes we feel sad that God has allowed us to go through difficult times. Don't be angry when this happens. A good father doesn't let his child get into trouble – he corrects him so that he will thank him for it later. So it is with God.

Even if it seems painful at the time, later we will realize we were saved from worse things because God has taught us many things through our struggles.

So don't be sad! Focus on what God is trying to do in your life and help one another.

Thank you, Lord, that you are the best father ever – and you want the very best for us.

Have you ever wanted to give up?

Remembering what Jesus suffered for us can help.

 Hebrews 12:1-4

Many people of faith have lived and died before we were even born. They may have had more problems even than us — yet they trusted God. We need to be brave just like them!

It's a bit like running a race. We need to throw off anything that gets in the way of following Jesus and turn our backs on the bad things we keep doing that slow us down.

We need to keep our eyes fixed on Jesus who went through the horrible pain of death on a cross. He knew that his suffering was worth it to be with God at the end. Think about that when you are tempted to give up. The way you feel will never be as bad as his suffering!

I want to follow you, Lord… help me when it seems too hard.

How much do we love God?

Do we find it hard to love God with all our hearts all the time?

 Revelation 2:1-5

God once spoke to John in a vision asking him to write to the Christians in Ephesus to remind them of their commitment.

'I know how many good things you are doing,' says God. 'I have seen how hard you work and how patient you are. I have seen how important the truth is in your lives and how you have suffered but not given up.

'Yet there is one thing wrong: once you loved me with all your heart. Your first love was very special. Come back to me now and love me as you once did. Don't let your love grow cold.'

Light a fire in our hearts, Lord, so our love does not grow cold.

365

Keep on keeping on…

Do we forget sometimes that all good things come from God who loves us?

 *Revelation 3:14-20*

God once spoke to John in a vision asking him to write to the Christians in Laodicea.

'I know you well and you are neither hot nor cold but merely lukewarm. You say, "I am rich and I have everything I want; I am so lucky!" You don't seem to realize that inside you are poor and blind and naked.

'Ask me to help you. Open your eyes to what is really happening. Come to me and seek my blessing again. I am like a father who tells his child when he is going the wrong way – because he loves him.

'Look! I am at the door, knocking. Can you hear me? Open the door so that I can come in and stay with you.'

Come into our lives, Lord, and help us to see your many blessings.

Reading in Bible Order

Here are the stories and passages in the order of the Bible for those who might prefer to read The Family Bible in this way.

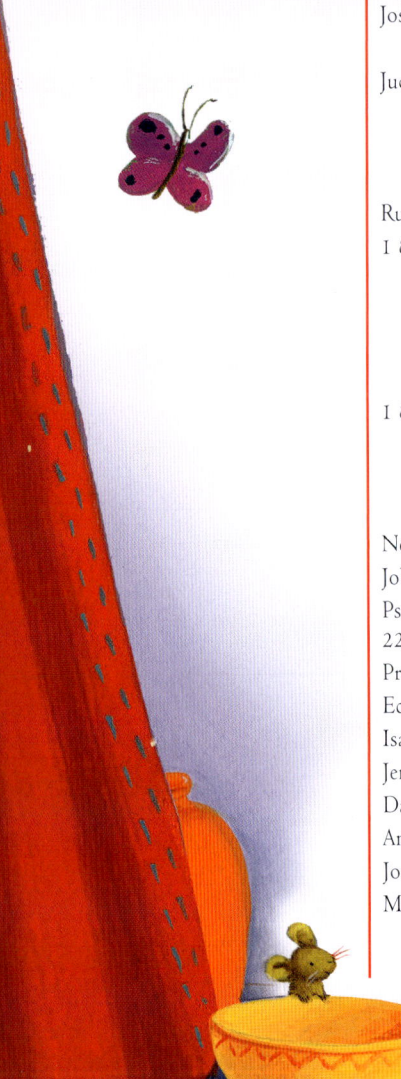

Old Testament

Genesis
    The story of creation 9-14
    Cain and Abel 46
    Noah 48-51
    Abraham 52-54, 56, 58-63
    Isaac 64-66
    Jacob 66, 70-76, 78-82, 84-85
    Joseph 96-111
Exodus
    Moses 120-143
Joshua
    Joshua 164-171
Judges
    Deborah 172-173
    Gideon 174-177
    Samson 178-179
Ruth 184-188
1 & 2 Samuel
    Hannah 202-203
    Samuel and Saul 204-211
    Samuel and David 212-214
    David 216-224, 226
1 & 2 Kings
    Solomon 226-229
    Elijah 254-261
    Elisha 262-263
Nehemiah 284-287
Job 86-87
Psalms 7, 8, 16-17, 22, 77, 161, 225, 265
Proverbs 4-6
Ecclesiastes 1-3
Isaiah 55, 112-119
Jeremiah 264, 266-271
Daniel 272-283
Amos 360
Jonah 88-95
Micah 241

New Testament

Gospels, Matthew, Mark, Luke and John
    The Christmas story 26-33, 34-37
    John the Baptist 24-25, 145-144
    Jesus' childhood 38-39
    Baptism of Jesus 146
    Jesus is tested 147
    Jesus ministry 148-160, 162-3, 190-201, 230-240, 242-253, 288-289
    The Easter story 290-309, 314-322
Acts
    The Ascension 323
    Pentecost 326-327
    The early church 330-353
Romans 15, 21, 189, 324, 354
1 & 2 Corinthians 301, 355-358, 47, 359
Galatians 299, 328
Ephesians 40, 67, 83
Philippians 310-313
Colossians 68-69, 325
2 Timothy 23
Hebrews 18-19, 57, 363, 362
James 180-183, 329
1 Peter 361
I John 41-45
Revelation 215, 364-365

Index

A
Aaron 126, 127, 128, 129, 131, 139, 140
Abednego 272, 273, 277, 278
Abel 46
Abraham 52, 53, 54, 56, 57, 58, 61, 62, 63, 64, 85, 328
Abraham's servant 64, 65
Adam 11, 13, 14
Ahab 254, 255, 257, 258
Altar 24, 51, 258, 259
Amos 360
Ananias 339, 340
Andrew 151
Angel, angels 18, 25, 29, 31, 32, 37, 57, 59, 60, 63, 75, 82, 147, 169, 174, 175, 278, 283, 317, 323, 343, 347
Angel of death 131
Anger 37, 46, 74, 83, 95, 109, 123, 127, 140, 155, 181, 225, 325, 334
Animals 7, 9, 10, 11, 48, 49, 50, 51, 52, 53, 54, 81, 87, 131, 174, 178, 217, 282, 292
Anna 33
Annunciation 26
Anointing 193, 208, 213, 226, 290
Anxiety 132, 244
Ararat, Mount 50
Arguments 4
Ark 48, 49, 50, 51
Ark of the Covenant 142, 219
Artaxerxes 284, 285, 287
Assurance 19
Assyrians 88

B
Baal 254, 258
Babies 24, 26, 27, 28, 29, 30, 32, 33, 35, 53, 54, 56, 61, 66, 85, 120, 121, 122, 202, 203, 224, 228
Babylon 273
Babylonians 268, 269, 271
Baptism 144, 145, 146, 337, 340, 345, 349, 353, 355
Barabbas 306
Barak 172, 173
Barnabas 341
Baruch 267
Bathsheba 220, 222, 224
Beatitudes 154
Belshazzar 279, 281
Benjamin 85, 104, 107, 108
Bethany 244
Bethel 76, 85, 261
Bethlehem 30, 31, 32, 35, 36, 37, 85, 184, 185, 186, 212
Betrayal 294, 296, 303
Bible 22, 23, 204, 232, 267, 319
Birthright 70
Blame 14, 89, 257
Blasphemy 304
Blessings 53, 54, 63, 70, 71, 72, 73, 74, 75, 76, 82, 84, 85, 99, 120, 365,
Blindness 204, 271, 338, 339, 340
Boaz 186, 187, 188
Bread 5, 100, 230, 256, 300, 319
Brothers 46, 70, 73, 74, 82, 84, 96, 97, 98, 99, 104, 105, 106, 107, 108, 109, 111, 151, 217, 239
Bullies 59
Burial 248, 315, 316
Burning bush 125

C
Caesar Augustus 30
Caesarea 345
Caiaphas 304
Cain 46
Caleb 143
Camels 64, 98, 174
Cana 148
Canaan 52, 53, 104, 105, 108, 110, 111, 143, 164, 165, 171, 177
Capernaum 152, 191
Captives 272, 273
Care 9, 356
Carmel, Mount 257, 258
Celebrations 38, 148, 219, 279, 287, 295, 301, 326
Chariot of fire 261
Chariots 133
Cheating 73, 74, 79, 81, 247, 253, 292
Childhood 38
Childlessness 202
Children 4, 24, 53, 66, 67, 71, 73, 74, 75, 107, 111, 197, 220, 234, 250, 264, 365
Choices 14, 16, 65, 90, 124, 140, 141, 163, 208, 245, 258, 282, 327, 333, 353
Christmas story 26, 27, 29, 30, 31, 32
Circumcision 312
Comfort 55
Commitment 364
Compassion 153, 192
Confession 89, 113, 145, 223
Conversion 329, 333, 336, 337, 340, 345, 349
Corinth 47, 301, 355, 359
Cornelius 343, 344, 345
Courage 302, 350
Covenant 142
Creation 18
Crime 304, 306
Cross 15, 18, 41, 44, 307, 308, 310, 312, 314, 315, 324, 327, 328, 337, 353, 359
Crown of thorns 307
Crucifixion 307, 308, 309, 314, 315
Cruelty 54

D
Damascus 338, 339, 340, 341
Danger 189
Daniel 272, 273, 275, 276, 277, 279, 280, 281, 282, 283
Darius 281, 282, 283
David 30, 188, 213, 214, 216, 217, 218, 219, 220, 221, 222, 223, 224, 226, 265

Death 2, 15, 18, 85, 111, 131, 173, 179, 189, 192, 197, 214, 215, 226, 242, 248, 249, 254, 297, 308, 310, 314, 315, 334, 342, 346
Deborah 172, 173
Deceit 35, 118, 282
Delilah 178, 179
Depression 224, 260, 268
Desert 124, 126, 134, 136, 143, 144, 147
Devil 147
Difficulties 116, 180
Disappointment 79
Disasters 17, 86, 98, 99, 116, 120, 189, 268, 351
Disciple, disciples 151, 195, 197, 199, 231, 232, 234, 240, 291, 294, 295, 296, 300, 302, 303, 304, 309, 318, 319, 320, 323, 326, 332, 334, 338
Discipleship 151, 194, 252
Discipline 4, 67, 355
Dishonesty 118
Disobedience 13, 14, 88, 89, 112, 118, 139, 140, 172, 178, 181, 211
Donkey 207, 291
Doubt, doubts 29, 107, 110, 125, 339
Dreams 29, 36, 37, 75, 96, 97, 100, 101, 102, 104, 227, 273, 274, 275, 276
Dying 308

E
Earthquake 349
Easter Day 316, 317, 318, 319
Egypt 37, 38, 98, 99, 102, 103, 104, 107, 109, 110, 111, 120, 122, 131, 132, 166
Egyptians 123, 133, 139, 268
Eli 202, 203, 204,
Elijah 254, 255, 256, 257, 258, 259, 260, 261
Elimelech 184
Elisha 260, 261, 262, 263

Elizabeth 24, 25, 26, 27, 28, 144
Emmaus 319
Encouragement 29, 164, 180, 286, 287
Enemies 156, 362
Ephesus 364
Epiphany 34, 35, 36
Equality 328
Esau 66, 70, 71, 72, 73, 74, 82, 84, 85
Escape 37, 341, 347, 352
Eternal life 248
Ethiopia 337
Eve 11, 12, 13, 14
Execution 307, 346
Exile, exiles 272, 284
Ezra 287

F
Fairness 145, 238, 241, 360
Faith 1, 24, 25, 26, 29, 46, 47, 52, 62, 63, 86, 91, 119, 129, 143, 166, 170, 171, 175, 183, 191, 196, 216, 217, 218, 231, 248, 250, 256, 284, 286, 312, 317, 320, 327, 328, 329, 337, 341, 343, 345, 349, 350, 351, 353, 357
Faithfulness 142
Family, families 4, 18, 38, 43, 46, 49, 50, 51, 59, 64, 65, 66, 67, 68, 70, 71, 72, 73, 79, 81, 82, 85, 86, 87, 96, 104, 110, 111, 124, 170, 184, 185, 188, 197, 203, 239, 243, 256, 328, 343, 345, 349, 355, 362
Famine 102, 103, 104, 184
Fasting 118
Favourites 66, 71, 96, 345
Fear, fears 13, 17, 18, 30, 45, 89, 90, 93, 98, 110, 116, 123, 125, 126, 130, 133, 138, 143, 167, 169, 172, 195, 210, 215, 222, 231, 240, 274, 275, 279, 280, 283, 297, 304, 305, 318, 323, 325, 327, 351
Fiery furnace 277, 278
Fire 125, 259, 326

Fish 230, 321
Fishing 151, 195, 321
Fleece 175
Flight into Egypt 37
Flood 48, 50, 51, 133, 352
Flour 256
Food 5, 56, 66, 71, 72, 73, 74, 104, 107, 134, 135, 143, 145, 148, 160, 171, 186, 187, 197, 230, 244, 255, 272, 287, 288, 289, 344
Footwashing 295
Forgiveness 5, 15, 41, 69, 74, 83, 84, 88, 94, 106, 109, 113, 114, 117, 140, 141, 193, 222, 223, 226, 229, 235, 241, 243, 287, 301, 308, 312, 322, 327, 332, 334, 338, 345, 353
Frankincense 36
Freedom 15, 23, 38, 125, 128, 129, 132, 134, 346, 353
Friends 5, 11, 86, 109, 124, 148, 152, 153, 195, 199, 243, 248, 249, 294, 295, 296, 300, 303, 304, 305, 311, 326, 328, 338, 345
Friendship 5, 77, 84, 281, 327
Funeral 192
Future 1, 184, 185, 188

G
Gabriel 24, 25, 26
Galilee 150
Garden of Eden 11, 12
Garden of Gethsemane 302, 303
Gaza 337
Generosity 6, 47, 69, 75, 118, 145, 156, 157, 235, 238, 240, 293, 330, 343
Gideon 174, 175, 176, 177
Gifts 6, 36, 46, 96, 203, 227, 228, 230, 263, 275, 293, 333, 334, 357, 360
Giving 47, 157, 343, 357
Goats 52, 54, 78, 81
God, the creator 2, 8, 9, 10, 55, 161

God's
    blessings 26, 27, 86, 134, 154, 168, 171, 202, 203, 211, 220, 224, 225, 227, 228, 261, 273, 328
    care 91, 99, 107, 161, 187, 192, 217, 255
    children 43, 44
    commandments 3, 67, 137, 226
    family 40, 44, 116
    friends 2, 41
    greatness 115
    help 179
    kindness 40
    kingdom 194, 234, 238, 239, 245, 250, 345
    laws 16
    love 27, 43, 44, 45, 53, 69, 75, 117, 131, 150, 171, 172, 180, 189, 198, 214, 223, 237, 265, 287, 325, 336, 362
    patience 128, 175, 266
    plans 26, 28, 29, 40, 102, 104, 105, 109, 126, 128, 174, 188, 189, 204, 205, 208, 209, 213, 264, 265, 286
    power 166
    presence 7, 116, 164, 219
    promises 51, 56, 76, 82, 117, 119, 142, 143, 167, 323
    provision 135, 160
    voice 23, 125, 204
    word 22, 23, 204, 232, 267, 319
Gold 36
Golden calf 139, 140
Golgotha 307
Goliath 217, 218
Gomorrah 54, 58, 60, 61
Good Friday 314, 315
Goshen 110, 120
Gossip 5, 325, 329
Grace 15, 19, 40, 41, 238, 245, 308, 312, 324, 327, 337, 345, 353
Graveclothes 316
Greed 138, 145, 206, 220,

221, 222 280, 301
Grief 192, 197, 249, 317, 342
Grudges 69, 82, 83, 95, 225, 235, 262, 301, 358
Guests 57
Guidance 22, 64, 114, 118, 121, 124, 127, 132, 172, 177, 186, 189, 207, 209, 214, 311, 339, 357
Guilt 13, 14, 16, 106, 221, 222, 223, 224, 243, 322, 353

H
Hannah 202, 203
Happiness 41, 119, 138, 171, 203, 205, 211, 224
Haran 52, 78
Harp 216
Harvest 9, 46, 102, 103, 187, 242, 328
Hate, hatred 97, 99, 281, 334, 335
Healing 150, 153, 190, 196, 197, 225, 230, 246, 252, 263, 330, 332, 334, 336, 339, 340, 342, 352, 357
Heaven 18, 42, 75, 119, 214, 215, 240, 248, 251, 288, 297, 308, 323, 324, 325
Herod 24, 34, 35, 37
Herod Agrippa 346
Holy Communion 300, 301
Holy Spirit, the 45, 145, 146, 189, 323, 326, 330, 332, 337, 340, 344, 345, 355
Home 52, 75
Homeless, the 157, 245
Honesty 6, 35, 72, 145, 158, 170, 202, 222, 241, 360
Hope 22, 92, 105, 119, 268
Horeb, Mount 260
Hospitality 56, 59, 78, 118, 124, 244
Humility 241, 247, 310
Hunger 134, 135, 147, 174, 184, 189, 230, 288

I

Idols 137, 272, 279
Illness 86, 190, 191, 196, 248, 289
Injustice 358, 360
Isaac 61, 62, 63, 64, 65, 66, 71, 73, 74, 85
Isaiah 55, 112
Israel 85, 211
Israelites 38, 112, 114, 120, 123, 125, 132, 133, 134, 135, 136, 140, 143, 168, 170, 171, 172, 173, 174, 178, 205, 206, 210, 217, 218, 258, 287

J

Jacob 66, 70, 72, 73, 74, 75, 76, 78, 79, 80, 81, 82, 84, 85, 96, 98, 104, 107, 108, 110, 111
Jael 173
Jairus 196
James 151, 180, 302, 346
Jealousy 46, 96, 97, 137, 238, 281
Jehoiakim 267
Jeremiah 264, 266, 267, 268, 269, 270, 271
Jericho 165, 166, 167, 169, 170, 233, 252, 253
Jerusalem 33, 34, 38, 39, 171, 215, 219, 233, 268, 271, 272, 284, 285, 286, 287, 291, 292, 295, 326, 333, 336, 337, 339, 341, 350
Jesse 188, 212, 213
Jesus
    arrest 303, 304
    anointing 290
    ascension 18, 323
    baptism 146
    betrayal 294, 296, 303
    birth 18, 30
    burial 315
    calls disciples 151
    childhood 38, 39
    crucifixion 307, 308, 309, 314, 315, 327, 331, 337, 345
    death 15, 18, 314, 345
    denial by Peter 305
    example 182
    flight into Egypt 37
    goodness 19
    humanity 19
    humility 146, 291, 295, 310
    I am the gate 149
    I am the good shepherd 236
    I am the resurrection and the life 248
    I am the vine 298
    I am the way, the truth and the life 297
    incarnation 18, 19
    kingship 291, 310
    punishment 308, 324
    refugee 37
    resurrection 18, 312, 316, 317, 318, 319, 320, 321, 322, 323, 327, 331, 338
    Saviour 31, 32
    Son of God 39, 146, 248, 314
    suffering 302, 307, 308, 309, 310, 314
    temptations 147
    thanksgiving 33
    trial 304, 306
Jethro 124, 126
Jezebel 254, 257, 260
Job 86, 87
John 151, 215, 302, 309, 316, 330, 332, 364, 365
John Mark 346, 347
John the Baptist 24, 28, 144, 145, 146, 239
Jonah 88, 89, 90, 92, 93, 95, 264
Joppa 88, 342, 343, 344
Jordan 261
Joseph, Jacob's son 96, 97, 98, 99, 100, 101, 102, 103, 104, 105, 106, 108, 109, 110, 111, 120
Joseph, the carpenter 26, 29, 30, 32, 37, 38, 39, 150
Joseph of Arimathea 315
Joshua 143, 164, 165, 167, 168, 169, 170, 172
Journey, journeys 34, 37, 52, 64, 131, 132, 338, 342, 351, 353
Joy 7, 32, 33, 148, 203, 219, 246, 327, 354, 356
Judas 290, 294, 296, 300, 303, 339
Judgement 280, 288
Judges 172, 173, 174, 175, 176, 177, 178, 179
Judging others 122, 165, 182, 212, 290
Julius 351
Justice 55, 58, 96, 145, 182, 238, 241, 360

K

Kindness 5, 6, 19, 64, 69, 118, 138, 153, 154, 156, 166, 182, 185, 186, 188, 212, 225, 233, 235, 238, 240, 241, 262, 288, 292, 342, 362
King of
    Aram 262
    Babylon 272, 284
    Egypt 100, 101, 102, 103, 109, 120, 122, 123, 125, 126, 127, 128, 129, 130, 131, 133
    Israel 209, 213, 262, 263
    Judea 24, 35, 346
    Nineveh 94
    the Jews 307
Kish 207

L

Laban 74, 78, 79, 80, 81
Lake Galilee 26, 152, 154, 195, 231, 321
Lamb, lambs 46, 62, 114, 131
Laodicea 365
Last supper 296, 300, 301
Law, laws 38, 137, 138, 140, 141, 142, 164, 272, 282, 283, 287, 312
Lazarus 244, 248, 249, 290
Leader, leaders 164, 174, 207, 219, 286
Leah 79

Leper, lepers 190, 246
Leprosy 190, 246, 262
Levi 141
Lies 41, 42, 68, 72, 83, 137, 145, 247
Life 1, 22, 114, 115, 117, 149, 162, 199, 242
Light 22, 41, 42, 155
Listening 162, 163, 181, 244, 250, 337
Loneliness 181, 237, 260, 268, 323
Lot 52, 54, 59, 60
Love 3, 10, 11, 26, 42, 43, 44, 45, 57, 62, 68, 69, 78, 88, 108, 113, 130, 156, 157, 185, 193, 225, 232, 248, 250, 288, 290, 292, 293, 302, 305, 311, 322, 354, 357, 358, 361, 362, 364
Loyalty 166, 170, 185, 303, 358
Luke 351

M

Malta 352
Manna 135
Martha 244, 248, 249, 290
Martyr 334
Mary, mother of Jesus 26, 27, 28, 29, 30, 32, 33, 36, 37, 38, 39, 148, 309, 316, 290, 309
Mary Magdalene 314, 316, 317
Mary, sister of Lazarus 244, 248, 249, 290
Maundy Thursday 302
Mercy 58, 263
Meshach 272, 273, 277, 278
Micah 241
Midian 124
Midianites 174, 177
Miracle, miracles 61, 100, 126, 131, 133, 134, 168, 175, 176, 278, 318, 330, 331, 332, 333, 342, 347
    the catch of fish 151
    the healing of one man with a skin disease 190
    the healing of ten men with a skin disease 246

the feeding of the 5,000 230

the healing of the paralyzed man 152, 153

the healing of the soldier's servant 191

the healing of the woman with a haemorrhage 196

the raising of Jairus' daughter 197

the storm on the lake 195

the widow's son at Nain 192

water into wine at the wedding in Cana 148

the healing of the blind man 252

the raising of Lazarus 249

walking on water 231

Miriam 121, 122
Mistakes 89, 221, 222, 226, 243, 266, 287, 327
Moab 184, 186
Money 3, 6, 43, 86, 87, 98, 104, 106, 107, 179, 180, 242, 243, 251, 293, 296, 330, 333, 357
Moneychangers 292
Moses 121, 122, 123, 124, 125, 126, 127, 128, 129, 130, 131, 132, 133, 134, 135, 136, 138, 139, 140, 141, 142, 143, 164
Mount of Olives 302
Moving house 52
Murder 37, 46, 97, 123, 137, 220, 271, 334, 341
Myrrh 36

N

Naaman 262, 263
Nain 192
Naomi 184, 185, 186, 187, 188
Nathan 221, 222, 224
Nativity 30
Nazareth 26, 38, 150
Nebuchadnezzar 274, 275, 276, 277, 278, 279
Nehemiah 284, 285, 286, 287

Neighbour, neighbours 182, 232, 233,
New birth 198
Nicodemus 198, 315
Nile, River 101
Nineveh 88, 93, 94
Noah 48, 49, 50, 51

O

Obadiah 257
Obed 188
Obedience 22, 117, 127, 130, 142, 277, 311, 340
Old age 2, 3, 24, 52, 56, 71, 85, 111, 204, 206, 226, 261, 264, 279
Orpah 184, 185

P

Pain 86, 119, 127, 215, 308, 309, 325, 363
Palm Sunday 291
Parables
    buried treasure 194
    good Samaritan 233
    great feast and reluctant guests 245
    lost sheep 237
    loving father 243
    money lender 193
    Pharisee and the tax collector 247
    rich fool 242
    two sons 239
    unforgiving servant 235
    widow and the judge 159
    wise and foolish man 162, 163
    workers in the vineyard 238
Parents 4, 38, 66, 67, 71, 73, 74, 196, 197
Passover 38, 131, 291, 295, 306, 346
Patience 24, 54, 61, 101, 128, 180, 285, 323, 364

Paul, formerly Saul 15, 23, 40, 47, 67, 68, 83, 301, 310, 311, 312, 313, 335, 336, 338, 339, 340, 341, 348, 349, 350, 351, 352, 353, 354, 355, 359, 361
Peace 17, 33, 69, 136, 138, 174, 205, 219
Peacemakers 329
Pentecost 326, 327
Persecution 346
Perseverance 364, 365
Peter 151, 231, 235, 302, 304, 305, 316, 321, 322, 327, 330, 331, 332, 342, 343, 344, 345, 346, 347
Pharisees 193, 247, 312
Philip 337, 336
Philippi 310, 311, 348, 349
Philistines 178, 205, 217
Pillar of cloud 132
Pillar of fire 132
Plagues 128, 129, 130, 131
Plots 282, 294, 341
Poor, the 6, 30, 113, 145, 150, 157, 182, 183, 240, 245, 251, 271, 287, 290, 293, 296
Pontius Pilate 306, 315, 331
Potiphar 99
Power 96, 147, 222, 261, 276, 281, 313, 326, 327, 330, 360
Praise 27, 92, 246, 348, 360
Prayer, prayers 24, 38, 61, 64, 65, 89, 92, 93, 113, 118, 119, 121, 125, 130, 135, 158, 159, 174, 189, 202, 203, 224, 229, 247, 258, 275, 276, 282, 284, 285, 286, 292, 300, 302, 303, 333, 337, 339, 342, 343, 344, 346, 347, 352, 357
Pride 157, 247, 252, 263, 280, 282
Priest, priests 19, 141, 190, 233, 246, 294, 304, 305, 306
Princess 121, 122
Prison 57, 99, 100, 101, 102, 105, 179, 268, 288, 289, 331, 332, 335, 336, 338, 346, 347, 348, 349, 350

Prisoner, prisoners 262, 272, 273, 306
Promised land 111
Prophecies 24, 337
Prophet, prophets 18, 88, 89, 205, 221, 241, 257, 258, 260, 263, 264, 291
Punishment 88, 95, 106, 108, 114, 224, 308, 324
Purpose 1, 3, 269, 313, 333, 363

Q

Quails 135

R

Rachel 78, 79, 80, 85, 96
Rahab 165, 166, 167, 170
Rain 49, 50, 254, 255, 257
Rainbow 51
Ravens 255
Rebekah 65, 66, 71, 72, 73, 74
Red Sea 133, 134
Refugee, refugees 37
Relationships 74, 82
Religious leaders 153, 193, 198, 291, 292, 294, 303, 304, 306, 308, 332, 334
Repentance 94, 106, 108, 113, 117, 145, 253
Respect 4, 57, 67, 137, 232, 261, 279, 311, 335
Responsibility 38
Resurrection 248, 316, 317, 327
Reuben 97, 107
Revenge 105, 156
Rhoda 347
Riches 6, 86, 242, 251, 365
Rivalry 234
River Jordan 54, 144, 145, 146, 164, 167, 168, 255, 263
River Nile 120, 121, 128
Rome 15, 354
Rules 3, 12, 16, 42, 77, 136, 137, 139, 222, 312
Ruth 184, 185, 186, 187, 188

S

Sabbath 137, 315, 316
Sacrifice 44, 62, 63, 113, 241, 259, 300, 354
Sadness 29, 57, 85, 98, 154, 192, 202, 215, 223, 224, 270, 317
Sailors 89, 90, 91
Samaria 199, 232, 336
Samaritan, Samaritans 199, 246
Samson 178, 179
Samuel 204, 205, 206, 207, 208, 209, 210, 211, 212, 213
Sarah 52, 53, 54, 56, 61
Saul, King 207, 208, 209, 210, 211, 216, 217, 218, 219
Saying sorry 74, 82
Self 15
Self control 329
Selfishness 81, 180, 310, 325, 359
Sermon on the Mount 155, 156, 157, 158, 160, 162, 163
Shadrach 272, 273, 277, 278
Shame 13, 14, 117, 226, 243, 305, 322
Sharing 6, 27, 47, 57, 93, 118, 230, 301, 332, 333, 336, 350, 353
Sheep 31, 32, 52, 54, 78, 81, 114, 125, 149, 213, 236, 237
Shepherd, shepherds 31, 32, 114, 124, 149, 214, 219, 236, 237
Shipwreck 352
Signs 131, 175
Silas 348, 249
Simon of Cyrene 307
Simeon 33, 106, 107
Simon the Pharisee 193
Simon the tanner 342, 344
Sinai, Mount 136
Sins 13, 15, 40, 41, 112, 113, 114, 116, 139, 144, 145, 146, 223, 224, 225, 229, 241, 281, 312, 314, 324, 345, 353
Sisera 172, 173

Slaves 98, 109, 120, 123, 125, 128, 130, 133, 217, 348
Sodom 54, 58, 60, 61
Soldier, soldiers 30, 120, 121, 165, 167, 173, 176, 191, 217, 219, 220, 262, 303, 307, 315, 318, 343, 345, 346, 347, 351
Solomon 1, 2, 3, 4, 5, 6, 224, 226, 227, 228, 229, 254
Sorrow 148
Spies 143, 165, 166, 167, 170
Star 31, 34, 36
Starvation 270
Stealing 4, 73, 137, 149, 221, 222, 253, 292, 360
Stephen 334, 335
Stocks 348
Stoning 334, 350
Storms 89, 90, 91, 195, 351, 352
Strangers 57, 58, 59, 186, 187, 188, 363
Strength 55
Suffering 19, 23, 86, 87, 119, 197, 215, 249, 302, 307, 308, 309, 314, 350, 356, 364

T

Tabitha 342
Tarshish 88
Tarsus 339
Tax collector, collectors 247, 253
Temple 229, 271
Temptation, temptations 12, 15, 19, 147, 180
Ten Commandments 137, 141, 142, 168, 171, 211, 222, 247, 254, 264, 272
Testing 280
Thanksgiving 7, 33, 46, 51, 69, 92, 184, 246, 276, 287, 301, 330, 354
Thief 308
Thirst 134, 199, 256
Thomas 297, 320
Time 244
Timothy 23
Tomb 315, 316

Trouble 5, 95, 116
Trust 1, 6, 24, 26, 27, 49, 62, 63, 84, 86, 91, 100, 119, 128, 132, 133, 134, 135, 140, 143, 166, 167, 169, 171, 172, 173, 180, 195, 214, 218, 231, 250, 256, 264, 268, 271, 283, 297, 312, 317, 329, 339, 351
Truth 34, 258, 358, 364

U

Unity 356
Uriah 220
Uzziah 112

V

Values 60, 206
Victory 173
Vision, visions 25, 215, 339, 344, 345, 364, 365

W

Waiting 54, 61, 285
Water 5, 11, 53, 64, 65, 134, 143, 148, 199, 214, 255, 259, 261, 272, 289, 337
Weakness 19, 30, 138, 140, 147, 179
Weariness 55
Well, wells 64, 65, 78, 97, 98, 124, 199, 269, 270,
Whirlwind 261
Widows 113, 181, 192, 255, 256, 293
Wife, wives 50, 52, 60, 64, 65, 78, 79, 80
Wind 326
Wine 100, 148, 272, 300
Wisdom 162, 212, 227, 228
Wise men 34, 36, 101, 276
Works 183
Worry 25, 29, 38, 39, 84, 132, 139, 158, 160, 195, 210, 244, 252, 283, 325, 342
Worship 6, 7, 18, 31, 34, 35, 36, 92, 113, 118, 130, 137, 139, 141, 147, 229, 254, 257, 258, 277, 287, 292, 320, 334, 346

Z

Zacchaeus 253
Zarephath 255, 256
Zechariah 24, 25, 26, 28, 144
Zedekiah 268

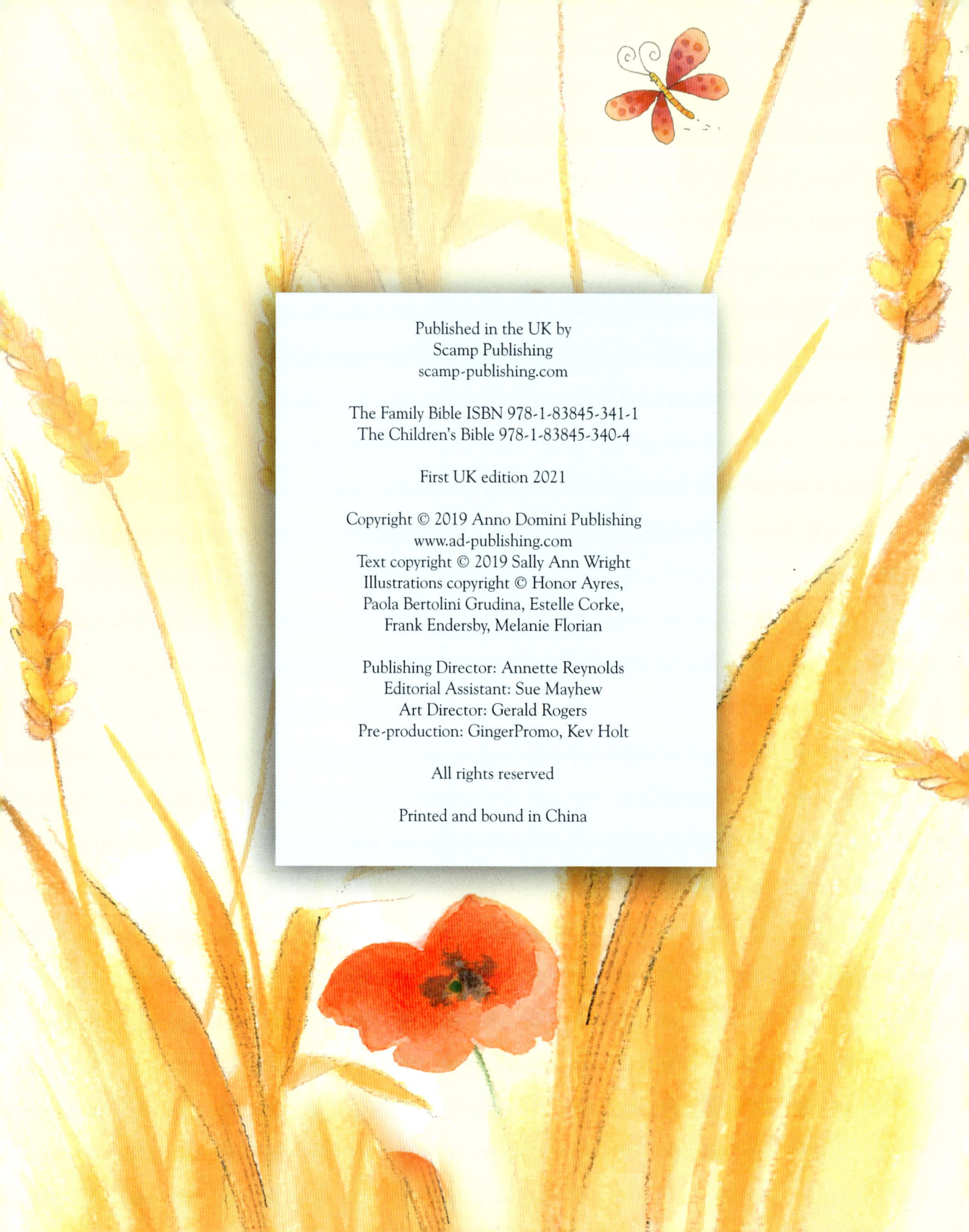

Published in the UK by
Scamp Publishing
scamp-publishing.com

The Family Bible ISBN 978-1-83845-341-1
The Children's Bible 978-1-83845-340-4

First UK edition 2021

Copyright © 2019 Anno Domini Publishing
www.ad-publishing.com
Text copyright © 2019 Sally Ann Wright
Illustrations copyright © Honor Ayres,
Paola Bertolini Grudina, Estelle Corke,
Frank Endersby, Melanie Florian

Publishing Director: Annette Reynolds
Editorial Assistant: Sue Mayhew
Art Director: Gerald Rogers
Pre-production: GingerPromo, Kev Holt

All rights reserved

Printed and bound in China